what i need **2** SUCCEED

what i need 2 SUCCEED

FROM A TO Z FOR TEENS

LINDA CARTER

with illustrations by Tina Cargile

New York

what i need 2 SUCCEED
FROM A TO Z FOR TEENS

© 2017 Linda Carter.

Published in New York, New York, by Morgan James Publishing. Morgan James and The Entrepreneurial Publisher are trademarks of Morgan James, LLC. www.MorganJamesPublishing.com

The Morgan James Speakers Group can bring authors to your live event. For more information or to book an event visit The Morgan James Speakers Group at www.TheMorganJamesSpeakersGroup.com.

Shelfie

A **free** eBook edition is available with the purchase of this print book.

CLEARLY PRINT YOUR NAME ABOVE IN UPPER CASE

Instructions to claim your free eBook edition:
1. Download the Shelfie app for Android or iOS
2. Write your name in **UPPER CASE** above
3. Use the Shelfie app to submit a photo
4. Download your eBook to any device

ISBN 978-1-63047-886-5 paperback
ISBN 978-1-63047-887-2 eBook
ISBN 978-1-63047-888-9 hardcover
Library of Congress Control Number:
2015919319

Cover Design by:
Rachel Lopez
www.r2cdesign.com

Interior Design by:
Bonnie Bushman
bonnie@caboodlegraphics.com

In an effort to support local communities and raise awareness and funds, Morgan James Publishing donates a percentage of all book sales for the life of each book to Habitat for Humanity Peninsula and Greater Williamsburg.

Get involved today, visit
www.MorganJamesBuilds.com

To my children and grandchildren, you've given me tremendous joy and you are the reasons I'm putting my thoughts into print.

To my husband, a chapter in this book should be dedicated to you because you truly are a success story—in business, with your family, and in life.

To my husband's sisters from whom I've learned much.

In memory of my mother, who had a quote for every occasion.

And, to the MacVicar Clan,
"Lang may yer lum reek."
(May you live long and happily.)

Table of Contents

Foreword

Most of us have used a GPS on our phone or in our car. By following its directions, we reach our destination. Well, this book is a teen's GPS for success and a better life.

You are now getting ready for the big show that is adulthood! Just as a GPS is a system of nearly 30 satellites that guarantee you will get where you are going, *What I Need 2 Succeed* is a system of 26 character traits that will lead you on a road to a purposeful and successful career.

Take my word; these elements will guide you to a rewarding life. It is not a cure for the ups and downs and detours you will face on the way, but it will act as a road map that will allow you to overcome most obstacles. Why do I believe this? Because I have used every one of them in my life time and have firsthand experience with what it takes to be successful.

Who am I? Well, I grew up on a farm in Missouri, a farm boy that learned the hard way. I was in the military during World War II and The Korean War and achieved the rank of Major in the United

States Marine Corp Reserve. After serving my country, I graduated from college and joined Mobil Oil Corporation (before it became Exxon Mobil) in petroleum marketing for a career of 36 years in various management positions. I was a very successful Field Manager for them and was responsible for the most successful major retail acquisitions in the history of Mobil. I've been working in the petroleum business for 65 years, now as a consultant. It has been a great career. I consider myself successful in life and in business because I lived by the principles you will learn about by reading this book.

While with Mobil, I was manager for all of Florida and Georgia, and worked with over 1,000 people. I can tell you those with good character traits were the 100 plus that I promoted to higher positions. Take time now to think about your educational progress thus far. Sure, you've learned the basics—the 3 R's of **R**eading, w**R**iting, and a**R**ithmatic. Let's go beyond that and learn what it takes to be a success.

For me, the most important traits a person can have are the 3 T's of **T**rustworthiness, hones**T**y, and a good a**T**titude because without these three, nothing else will work. Having lived 93 years, I can tell you that life goes by very quickly. Live a valued life and make the most of every minute.

You want to succeed, you want to enjoy life, and you want a good adult life. Take these principles into your heart and mind and live by them. The dividends they pay in your life will be well worth the effort.

John R. Moreland, Major
Ret. USMCR
Ret. District Manager, Mobil Oil Co.
Ft. Lauderdale, Florida
Born June 22, 1923

Preface

When high school students walked through the door of my classroom on the first day of school, I always wondered what was going on in their minds. Were they thinking of school or something else? Occasionally, I would find out what tremendous problems they were actually going through. Sometimes I would see them after they graduated, and their transformations were amazing! That's when I realized that these teenagers, with all their insecurities, can and will not only survive, but thrive, provided they are given the tools to do so. That, in a nutshell, is the purpose of this book.

Let's face it, teenage years are tough. It's a time of physical, mental, and emotional growth. They have many choices to make from deciding how their friends will influence them to what they will become as distinct adults. While teen years are exciting and fun, they can also be filled with uncertainty and fear. As teenage days yield to young-adulthood, paths must be chosen. They will soon face a fork in the road where they must choose between Dead-End Avenue or Success Street?

Why do some young adults emerge from the turbulent teenage years as winners while others appear destined not to succeed? What separates the two? The answer lies in the character traits of the individual. This book will help open teens' and young adults' minds to becoming more aware of their own character traits, skills, and talents so that they can explore careers that suit them. In this book the reader will see how personal challenges, problems, and difficulties can actually lead a person in the direction of Success Street.

The chapters of *WIN 2 Succeed* highlight famous people; there is something to learn from each of them. Sure, we've all read about their inventions, their writings, and their leadership skills; but what you will learn in this book are the hurdles they've overcome. In many instances, it was a small, seemingly insignificant event that put them on the road to success. They had failures, but at least they were trying! Their secret was not to rest on the failure but to get up and try again! Most of these famous individuals started life just like us, but they had perseverance and the willingness to work hard. That alone is what made them stand out.

Given the same set of circumstances, see if you would have been able to achieve what they did? Do you have it in yourself to change your current situations? I invite you to explore how you, too, can turn struggles into successes. The chapters of this book start with attitude and end with you!

Acknowledgements

I thank God for the opportunity to help teenagers. It was only with His guidance, that this book was written.

I thank my husband, Bob, my inspiration and best friend, for always supporting me and helping make my dreams come true.

I thank my daughter, Leigh McKinnon, a successful businesswoman and wonderful mother to Hadley and Jackson, who still always had the time to read my notes, give advice and words of encouragement, not only on this project but always.

I thank Tina Cargile, artist, for her wonderful drawings.

I thank Heidi Ross, a fantastic English teacher and my good friend. Thank you for your hard work. Going to press would not have been possible without your help.

I thank the Carter boys for being good teenagers. It is my prayer you find success in all your endeavors.

And I thank you for reading this book.

CHAPTER 1

Attitude

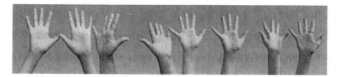

"Our greatest weakness lies in giving up. The most certain
way to succeed is always to try just one more time."
—Thomas A. Edison

Thomas Edison failed thousands of times before he revolutionized
the world by inventing and patenting the light bulb. During
his four-year quest to invent the incandescent light bulb,
Edison maintained an amazing positive attitude. About his electric light
experiments, he said "I was never myself discouraged or inclined to be
hopeless of success." Edison knew that he could find a way to make it
work! When interviewed by a young reporter who boldly asked Mr.
Edison if he felt like a failure, Edison replied, "Young man, I have not

failed. I've just found 10,000 ways that won't work. Success is almost in my grasp." And shortly after that, his experiment finally worked and the light bulb was invented.[1]

Although successful later in life, Edison did not have an easy childhood. Surprisingly, he had little formal education because his mother had to withdraw him from public school due to what some thought were learning difficulties. He did not even learn to talk until he was four years old. Then he constantly asked questions. A curious mind was developing.

Edison had severe hearing loss since childhood. He became totally deaf in his left ear and 80% deaf in his right ear, but his deafness apparently enabled him to block out distractions, thereby shaping his unique ability to concentrate. His lack of hearing prevented him from taking advantage of the benefits of a secondary education, but he never let it interfere with finding ways of compensating. As a matter of fact, this disability led to his success.

He developed a highly individualistic style of acquiring knowledge and read every book he could get his hands on, particularly books about science. Edison was not bitter that he could not attend college. He had the attitude that if he could not go to college, then college could come to him. He was, therefore, self-taught.

As a young adult, Edison worked in the telegraph industry. He spent much of his time working on and thinking of inventions, which led to his being fired by Western Union. Deeply in debt, Edison borrowed money from a friend to purchase a ticket to New York City, where he thought he might have more opportunities to peddle his inventions.

He was not an instant success. As a matter of fact, an amazing coincidence came at the lowest point in his life. As the penniless, twenty-

---

1   Beals, Gerald. "Edison Biography" http://www.thomasedison.com/biography.
html

some-year old Edison walked aimlessly through some of the offices in New York City's financial district; he noticed a crowd had gathered at a brokerage house. The stock-ticker machine had just broken down, and no one had a clue as to how to fix it. Being inquisitive, Edison seized the opportunity to see what was wrong with the machine. After spending just a few seconds confirming exactly how the stock ticker was supposed to work, he reached down and manipulated a loose spring back to where it belonged. To everyone's amazement, the device began to work again. The office manager was so ecstatic that he hired Edison on the spot at a salary of three hundred dollars per month. That was twice the going rate for a top electrician at the time.[2]

You see, Edison liked to tinker with things to see how they worked and he had an exceptional ability to concentrate. The manager no doubt was irritated and distracted by the crowd, but Edison remained calm while he analyzed the machine. The solution was not rocket science, just a simple bent spring! That event changed his life because he now had the means to pay for his experiments! There's a lesson to be learned here, think clearly, avoid distractions, and take advantage of opportunities whenever and wherever they arise.

Edison held a world record of 1093 patents for inventions. He came up with a meaningful new patent every two weeks throughout his working career. Quite a success story—simply because he remained calm and focused, had a goal and, most importantly, a positive attitude.

What can we learn from Thomas Edison? He was persistent. He did not think that any of his failed experiments were actually failures. Each experiment that did not work was viewed as just one more step in the right direction. How often do we give up after just one or two attempts? Never losing sight of the goal set before him, Edison kept trying even after 10,000 failed attempts. The reason then for his success was his positive attitude—he viewed each failure as progress and never quit. He said, "Our greatest weakness lies in giving up. The most certain way to succeed is always to try just one more time."

If you think back, you had a similar positive attitude when you were a small child. When at first you didn't succeed, you kept trying. It took many attempts to learn to crawl, to walk, and to ride a bicycle. You didn't give up then. And as a small child, you were probably also cheerful.

Do you still have that cheerful, never-give-up attitude? Your outlook will affect all aspects of your life—your personality, your relationships, and your career. Satisfaction in life and success in whatever it is you are doing will depend, to a considerable extent, on your attitude. It will have a significant effect on your career and overall happiness. You can make the choice today to either have a positive outlook on life or a negative attitude. Which will you choose?

Why do people behave the way they do? Why do some people have positive attitudes and others negative attitudes? The way you behave may have something to do with how you feel about yourself, your self-concept. Some people are so demanding of themselves that they are never quite satisfied with what they accomplish. They may even talk to themselves in a negative way—I'll never be able to do this; I'll never succeed, and so on.

Self-talk is made up of all our negative and positive thoughts. These thoughts are stored in our subconscious mind and affect our behavior. So, how do we change these negative feelings about our self-identity? One way is by changing the way we talk to ourselves. When you feel a negative idea coming on in your mind, quickly change it to a positive one.

Remember that negative people and whiners will always find reasons to be unhappy and will drag you down. Don't let them. It is much better to surround yourself with positive influences. The wonderful thing about attitude is that if you really want to, you can make an attitude adjustment. It's not at all difficult. All you have to do is change the way you think about things and how you view yourself.

Positive thinking is a mental attitude that sees the bright side of things. Start thinking upbeat thoughts today. With a positive attitude you will be able to visualize the results you want to achieve. You will be successful in life if you adopt the same approach as Edison. Learn from failures and mistakes. Be persistent. Be positive. Always keep your goal in sight.

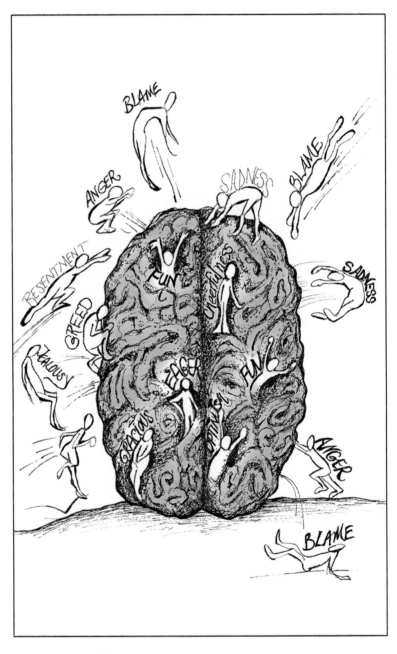

Change negative thoughts to positive ones

CHAPTER 2

Believe

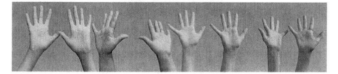

"When you believe in a thing, believe in it all the way, implicitly and unquestionable."

—Walt Disney

Walt Disney was born in 1901 and died in 1966—one year before construction began on Walt Disney World Resort in Florida. His brother Roy Disney inaugurated the Magic Kingdom on October 1, 1971. Disney had a very early interest in art; and as a child, his neighbor paid him to draw pictures of his horse Rupert. Drawing Rupert the horse was a significant event because that childhood experience gave him the idea to draw animals; and we all know about his most famous animation. Disney said, "He popped out of my mind onto a drawing pad 20 years ago on a train ride from Manhattan to Hollywood at a time when business fortunes of my brother Roy and myself were at a lowest ebb and disaster seemed right around the corner."[3]

From that drawing pad, Mickey Mouse was born! Well, almost. Mickey was originally "Mortimer Mouse" until Lillian Disney, Disney's wife, convinced him to change the name. His first role as Mickey was in Steamboat Willie, an animated short film.[4]

Steamboat Willie, who made its debut in 1928, was notable for being one of the first cartoons with synchronized sound. The sound in earlier short films was not perfected because the sound did not always match the motion. Steamboat Willie was produced using a new technique called click track where marks were made on the film to indicate precise timings for musical accompaniment. For the first time, sound effects were on target, and Steamboat Willie was an instance success. Everyone fell in love with Mickey Mouse.

A simple drawing led to a multi-billion dollar business all because Disney believed that a mouse could change the entertainment industry. He had a vision and Mickey Mouse was a means to an end; the improved sound effects also added to Mickey Mouse's success.

Disney made the most of something he enjoyed doing—drawing. A childhood hobby became an empire simply because Walt believed in his dream. He believed that an animated mouse could be his ticket to success. And was it ever! The Walt Disney Company now has annual revenues of approximately $35 to $45 billion.

Drawing was Disney's passion. What is your passion? How do you enjoy spending your time? Considering the fact that you will work about 80,000 hours over your lifetime, why not work at something you

3   "Walt Disney Quotes" http://www.justdisney.com/walt_disney/quotes/quotes01. html

4   "Hey Kids, Meet Walt Disney (Biography) http://makingartfun.com/htm/f-maf-art-library/walt-disney-biography.htm

enjoy. There are tens of thousands of different jobs. Make it a point as a teenager to find a part-time job doing something that interests you.

Ok, so maybe flipping burgers is not that enjoyable. What you may not realize is that a lot of successful people, who own restaurant franchises, making big bucks, actually started out flipping burgers part-time as a teenager. Don't ever think your menial job is a dead-end street. If you're with a good company, especially one that is growing, the opportunities are endless. Whatever your job is, learn all you can about it, and make the most of it. Believe that your current job is a stepping stone to a higher paying job. You never know where it may lead.

Disney is proof that hobbies, interests, and talents can become careers. Sure, he probably had some natural talent, but many hobbies can be learned if you have the interest. It is important to be good at what you do, and oftentimes, that takes practice. But if you want to be successful, the time spent honing your skills will pay off in the future. Besides, having hobbies keeps you out of trouble, right? Who knows, you may be the next Walt Disney!

Disney knew he was a good artist; he believed in himself. He said, "When you believe in a thing, believe in it all the way, implicitly and unquestionable." In other words, without a shred of doubt, believe in yourself and in your ability to do well. Believing in something implicitly means believing in it totally without reservation. That means to put forth your total effort. Looking at this statement from another angle is doing things half-heartedly or half way will *not* yield good results. A job well done requires total effort and hard work. Truly believe that your tasks are worthwhile because in doing so, you will find fulfillment. We are meant to have a satisfying and happy life.

Try believing in something with all your heart and see how things will fall into place. Disneyland, Disney World, and Disney movies and all that go along with them didn't just happen! Disney said he went through four steps: First, think; second, believe; third, dream; and finally, dare! Probably the most important step is to believe. If you fall short on the belief level, then it will never happen because confidence is essential. You can have all the dreams in the world but unless you believe you can accomplish them and then dare to do something about them, they are just dreams drifting through your mind. Follow these four steps and there's nothing you can't do. To repeat, think, believe, dream, and dare.

We were all born with creative abilities, gifts, and talents. Make a list of those things you believe about yourself. List all of them whether they are large or small. I'll bet you will discover that you are more talented than you thought.

And this brings us to jealously. Never be jealous that someone is smarter or better looking than you or who has a talent you wished you had. Chances are you have an ability, gift, or talent that others wish *they* had. A line in a poem called "Desiderata" by Max Ehrman goes like this, "If you compare yourself with others, you may become vain and bitter; for always there will be greater and lesser persons than yourself." Good words to live by.

Believing in yourself means that you have confidence in who you are. Successful people never doubt themselves or their ability to do well. Believe you can have success, and you will! You may wonder about how difficult the journey to success may be. Don't worry, just remember that, "If there's a will, there's a way!"

And when you start making big bucks, never lose sight of where you started. Even with his mass fortune, Walt Disney always remembered his humble beginnings because he often said, "I only hope that we don't lose sight of one thing—that it was all started by a mouse."

lieve

eve) **VERB**
ih-leev]

as truth
ire of the truth
'e faith,
nce, and trust

When you believe in something, believe in it implicitly.

CHAPTER 3

Communication

"A man's character may be learned from the adjectives which he habitually uses in conversation."
—Mark Twain

Mark Twain was born Samuel Clemens on November 30, 1830, the night of the Halley's Comet. As you know, Halley's Comet is visible from Earth every 75 to 80 years. Twain predicted his death—he said that he would die when Halley's Comet returned again. He was right.

When he was four, Twain moved with his family to Hannibal, Missouri. Hannibal, located on the Mississippi River, would later serve as a fictional town in his most famous books. When Twain turned eighteen,

the whitewashing was so ... , ,
and other items just to participate in the whitewashing. In 1889 Twain published *The Adventures of Huckleberry Finn*, which is considered by many to be a sequel of *The Adventures of Tom Sawyer*. These two works of art magically depict life along the Mississippi River in the 1800's. Mark Twain simply made famous his childhood memories—he wrote about his own adventures exploring the Mississippi River.

You could learn a lot from Tom Sawyer. He does get into trouble, but he is a born leader, and he goes through many adventures that change him. Events you have experienced in the past, even simple adventures, can help shape your future. They will become part of who you are.

Mark Twain had a love for the Mississippi River, a fact that was apparent in his books. It was easy for Twain to write about what was familiar to him. Who would have thought that books about two young boys' adventures would have remained major classics still being read 140 years later!

No doubt that Twain had a vivid imagination and a flair for writing. What is your flair? Are you good at writing, drawing, speaking; are you good at math or science? What is it you enjoy doing in your spare time? Explore your talents. They may be your ticket to success someday. Twain simply wrote about his childhood.

Writing, of course, is just one aspect of communication. Spoken communication is equally as important. How you say something is as important as what you say. Make sure you are communicating in a proper tone of voice and are enunciating each word so that you are understood by your listener. Practice speaking slowly and clearly in front of a mirror so you can see how your mouth forms words as you speak. Speak so that you can be heard.

Just as you walk without thinking, we also talk without thinking. However, being able to speak well is not only important, it will be vital for your success. Knowing how the body makes sound will help you improve your tone of voice. When we speak, changes are made in regular breathing. The power of your voice comes from air that is exhaled. Because you must sustain vibration in the voice box to generate sound, you inhale more swiftly and more deeply when speaking than in normal breathing.

Volume, or loudness, is the intensity of sound, and it depends upon the force of the air exerted. So when speaking, learn to control the amount of air you take in by using the muscles of the lower chest and stomach to exert more pressure (to talk louder) and to prolong air flow. Make a concentrated effort to have this air pressure coming from the lower chest and not from the neck or upper chest. Consider working on your voice volume by controlling this air flow if you speak either too loudly or too softly.

With practice, the way you speak can be improved. Slow down— take time to speak your words clearly and at an acceptable volume level. Surprise and please your parents, grandparents, or teacher by asking them to help you with your speech patterns. Have them analyze any difficulties you may have with your speaking abilities and then be willing to try to improve.

Also try some tongue twisters, such as Betty Botter bought some butter, but she said the butter's bitter. If I put it in my batter, it will make my batter bitter. But a bit of better butter will make it better than the bitter butter. So she bought a bit of better butter and put it in her batter. And her batter was not bitter!

Twain once said, "A man's character may be learned from the adjectives which he habitually uses in conversation." Twain even made that statement in the late 1800's at a time when 'adjectives used in conversation' were not nearly as colorful as today. What do people learn about you from the adjectives you use in conversation? Do you choose your words wisely and respectfully? Are you using foul words and slang expressions just to fit in? If so, stop.

It is no secret that inappropriate language is common in music and movies, but that still does not mean that it is acceptable. Just because you may hear certain words does not mean that you have to use them. You will be much more respected by your peers if you stick to high standards. Words do matter and you will be identified by the words you use. Evil communications corrupt good manners just as bad company corrupts good morals.

This is even more important today with social media. You are leaving an electronic footprint that will be impossible to erase. A good rule of thumb is: do not post anything you would not want your grandmother to see! College admissions offices and potential employers will Google your name. Would you be embarrassed about what they discovered you were posting online?

Fast forward twenty years. Accept as true the fact that you may be saddened you did not engage in more meaningful conversations with older family members when you had the chance. Twenty years from now, you may be disappointed that you did not go on that cross-country trip with your grandparents. Twenty years from now, you may be disappointed that you did not complete college. Sure you may have given up those things so that you could party with your friends; but parties come to a quick end while certain experiences last a lifetime.

When deciding what to do with your time, consider which option means the most to those who love you and what is best for your future.

Here's more Mark Twain wisdom: "Twenty years from now, you will be more disappointed by the things that you didn't do than by the ones you did do. So throw off the bowlines. Sail away from the safe harbor. Catch the trade winds in your sails. Explore. Dream. Discover."

CHAPTER 4

Dedication

"In order to excel, you must be completely dedicated to your chosen sport. You must also be prepared to work hard and be willing to accept criticism. Without 100 percent dedication, you won't be able to do this."

—Willie Mays

Dedication is the quality of being devoted or committed to something. On May 6, 1931, in Westfield, Alabama, Willie Mays, Jr. was born to Ann and Willie Howard Mays, Sr., who divorced when their son was three years old. Willie Junior was dedicated to the game of baseball. He began playing professional baseball shortly after the sport was desegregated. Mays was exceptional at both batting and fielding, and many consider him to be the greatest all-around player of all time.

According to his father, Mays learned to walk at the age of six months, and soon thereafter he and his father were playing catch with each other, with the father instructing his son in the basics of the game that would one day make him famous. His dad was determined that his son would not end up in the steel mills the way he did.

When Mays was growing up, his father played on a semi-professional baseball team sponsored by the mill. By age fourteen, he joined his father on the mill team. His high school had no baseball team, so he played basketball and football at school; but before he finished high school, it became clear that baseball would be his career. Mays began his professional career at age sixteen, playing with the Birmingham Black Barons in the segregated Negro Southern League. While his father avidly supported May's ambition to be a professional ball player, he also insisted his son finish high school. In his first year with the Barons, he was restricted to playing home games so he wouldn't miss school. The day he graduated from high school, he was signed by the New York Giants.

Mays got off to a rocky start in the majors, going hitless in his first twelve times at bat, but then Mays broke his hitless streak with a home run blasted over the left field roof. It took another thirteen times at bat for Mays to get his second major league hit, but he soon got the knack of hitting major league pitching and hit another nineteen home runs before the season was out.[5]

By the end of that season, he had been named "Rookie of the Year." Mays played for the Giants (which relocated to San Francisco in the late 1950s, becoming the San Francisco Giants) until 1972, when he was traded to the New York Mets.

---

5   Academy of Achievement."Willie Mays Biography." Baseball Hall of Fame. August 24, 2015. http://www.achievement.org/autodoc/printmember/may0bio-1

Willie Mays, Jr. often said that he owed his success to his dad. Even though he was from a broken home, his father was a tremendous influence in his life. He was not bitter that his parents did not stay together. There's an old saying that when life gives you lemons, make lemonade. In other words, make the best of a bad situation. Fourteen-year-old boys need their fathers; and Mays compensated for his dad not being at home by placing himself where his dad was—on the baseball field.

Research has shown that the key to the development of intelligence is in the child's experiences in the first three years—that is, during the period of development of the brain cells. Did you know that your brain has about 1.4 billion cells? As you grew, these cells linked and clung together to respond to and correlate information received from outside through the senses and this process is still ongoing. The period when the brain cells learn most rapidly to make these connections is the period between birth and three years of age.

That is exactly why Willie Mays was such an excellent baseball player. He learned to play baseball almost before he learned to walk. "As the tree is bent, so grows the tree" meaning whatever influences a child in infancy makes the deepest impression.

As a small child, Mays loved to play with a baseball. Try to remember the interests you had when you were young. Try them out again now that you are older. The things you learned even before elementary school will perhaps be the most prevalent in your life.

Willie Mays said it best when he said, "In order to excel, you must be completely dedicated to your chosen sport." That is true not only of sports, but in all of your endeavors. Whether it be school, work, sports, or extra-curricular activities, be dedicated to success—either individually or as a group.

He also said, "Be willing to accept criticism." In reality, you will want to know if you are doing something wrong so you can correct that area and improve. Consider the fact that criticism is often given to make a person better; don't take it personally. Then Mays went on to say, "Without 100 percent dedication, you won't be able to do this."

How do you approach your goals? If you find that you are not reaching them, then perhaps you are not giving it 100 percent. A casual approach will lead to mediocre results. A 100 percent dedicated approach will lead to fantastic results. If you want a better outcome, then put more time and effort into the activity. That means learning all you can about the endeavor and increasing the intensity of your practice.

There are many times when less than 100 percent dedication will not work. Think of it this way, would you want a surgeon to operate on you if he was less than 100 percent dedicated to performing a successful operation?

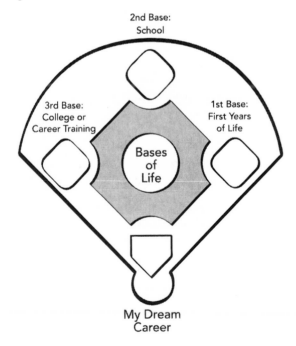

Bases of Life. Get a home run.

CHAPTER 5

Exploration

"Exploration: Equipped with his five senses, man explores the universe around him and calls this adventure Science."
—Edwin Powell Hubble

Explore your career interests. The man who was the inspiration behind the most powerful space telescope of the 20th century was about as confused as you are about what he wanted to be when he grew up.

Edwin Powell Hubble was born in 1889 in Missouri. He was a good student but was known more for athletics than intellectual abilities. He played baseball, football, basketball, and ran track in both high school and college.

Although his interest was always astronomy, he started his career teaching Spanish and math. He then went back to school to study law, fulfilling his dying father's wish. His law career was short-lived, and he went back to school to study physics and astronomy. After graduation, Hubble was invited to work at Mount Wilson Observatory in California but had to delay his acceptance while he served as a soldier in World War I.

When he returned to civilian life, he took a position at the observatory, but then left again in 1942 to serve in World War II. This skilled athlete and soldier, who also studied Spanish, math, physics, philosophy, law, and astronomy, was first to show that the universe is increasing and demonstrated that other galaxies besides our own Milky Way existed. It was the previous belief of many that space was limited to the Milky Way galaxy—Hubble's discoveries changed our view of the universe.

Because of his explorations and discoveries, the well-known Hubble Space Telescope is named after Edwin Hubble. It has provided valuable research data and images since it was carried into orbit in 1990, leading to many breakthroughs in the field of astrophysics. Hubble has also been honored with an asteroid and moon crater being named after him.

Hubble was lucky enough to be in the right place at the right time. Mount Wilson was the center for observational work of the universe and had the Earth's most powerful telescope, the 100-inch Hooker Telescope, of that time. Hubble's research, so brilliantly carried out between two world wars, had provided strong evidence for the need of a telescope larger than the 100-inch reflector. He assisted in the design of a 200-inch telescope.

When you are grown, you, too, can put yourself in the right place at the right time. Start now by identifying areas in which you have the necessary skills and knowledge that will allow you to take advantage of sudden opportunities when and if they arise. Not only be ready, but also look for those opportunities. After all, you cannot catch a fish without being close to water, right!

In 2015, to celebrate its 25th anniversary, the Hubble Telescope returned to the site of what may be its most famous image, the columns of the Eagle Nebula, and produced a stunning new picture. This "Pillars of Creation," located 6,500 light years away, was photographed using the telescope's upgraded equipment.[6] Look the image up on the World Wide Web; it is fantastic.

Hubble's two important discoveries—first, that Milky Way was not the only galaxy, and second, that the universe is expanding—both proved that two of his scientific rivals were wrong in their original theories. The first rival was a coworker, who became bitter and jealous that Hubble contradicted him by discovering other galaxies. The other rival was Albert Einstein himself!

Can you imagine the courage it took to prove that the famous Albert Einstein was wrong? This discovery was a tremendous breakthrough for astronomy of that time as it overturned the conventional view of a static universe and showed that the universe itself was expanding. More than a decade earlier, Einstein at first thought the universe was expanding but then corrected his equations to coincide with a static, non-changing universe. Now Hubble had demonstrated that Einstein's changed theory that was published was wrong and that Einstein's first theory was the correct one.

The world-famous physicist Einstein even paid Hubble a visit at Mount Wilson to express his gratitude for Hubble's discovery. Einstein called the original change of his beloved equations *"the greatest blunder of my life."*[7]

---

6   "NASA" https://www.nasa.gov/content/goddard/hubble-goes-high-definition-to-revisit-iconic-pillars-of-creation
7   https://www.spacetelescope.org/about/history/the_man_behind_the_name/

Despite Hubble's role in improving the existing understanding of the universe, he never received the Nobel Prize. Every year, prizes, called the Nobel Prizes, are given to people around the world for the study of science and for world peace. The science prizes include literature, science, and medicine. The Nobel Prize was started by Alfred Nobel when his 1895 testament (or will) gave money for the awards. The Nobel Foundation now controls the money. The Foundation asks different committees or academies to decide who receives this high honor. Each prize winner gets a medal, a diploma, and a sum of money.

Einstein received a Nobel Prize in 1922 for his discovery of the law of the photoelectric effect. But during Hubble's lifetime, astronomy was not considered a field of physics and therefore not science which would be eligible for the world-renowned Nobel Prize. But shortly after Hubble's death in 1953, the Nobel Prize Committee decided that astronomical work would be eligible for the physics prize. Since the Nobel Prize cannot be awarded after someone's death, Hubble was ineligible.

Something can be learned from Hubble's experience in proving that two of his scientific competitors were wrong. Work hard and do what you think is right—some friends or coworkers may be jealous of your success and others may be happy for you. That is life. So maybe you don't get a certain prize even though you think you deserve it. If you continue to do what is respectable, who knows an asteroid or moon crater may be named after you!

During his academic and beginning career days, Hubble had seven very different interests: being an athlete, serving in the military, teaching Spanish, teaching math, being a lawyer, studying physics and philosophy, and working as an astronomer. He was famous in the field that interested him the most—the study of the universe. The Hubble Telescope would have been named something entirely different if Hubble had remained a lawyer or a Spanish teacher.

Like Hubble, you also may change your mind about what you want to become after you complete your education. College costs these days are astronomical, so it is well worth your effort to explore career choices before you even enroll into a college or vocational program. College costs have risen 330% over the last twenty years, so it is important to decide on a college major early so that you will not have to spend more years and money than necessary trying to decide what you want to become.

Becoming more focused now will help you avoid the usual panic senior year of college when you must face the realization that you have no idea what the world of work holds for you. Open your mind to becoming more aware of your skills and talents so that you can explore careers that are right for you.

Reach for the stars

CHAPTER 6

Friends

"You can make more friends in two months by becoming interested in other people than you can in two years by trying to get other people interested in you."
—Dale Carnegie

ince you're in Chapter 6, let's try an experiment to see if you can outsmart your right foot! It's a neat trick to show your friends. While sitting down, lift your right foot off the floor and make clockwise circles with it. Good. Now, while still making these circles (be sure they're clockwise), draw the number "6" in the air with your right hand. Your foot will change direction!!

Dale Carnegie is best known for his 1936 book entitled *How to Win Friends and Influence People*. The principles contained in this book are still being taught today in leadership and public speaking seminars throughout the world. In this book, he discusses six ways to make people like you, such as being interested in others, smiling, and being a good listener.

You've probably heard the surname Carnegie as it was a famed family for which Carnegie Hall is named. Dale Carnegie was certainly not a member of that family. Quite the contrary; his family were impoverished farmers. The surname spelling was actually Carnagey; but when he published his first book, he changed the spelling to Carnegie. The new spelling made people associate his classes and books with the famous Carnegie family. Using a familiar name was a good marketing technique.

Unskilled in athletics, Carnegie learned at an early age that he could still make friends and earn respect because he had a way with words. He did not make the athletic team, so he joined the debate team. That decision put him on a course for success. If he couldn't make it on the playing field, then he would in the speaking arena.

You may think that the only way to be popular is to be an athlete or a cheerleader. That is simply not true, and Carnegie is proof the premise is wrong. He was popular because he was a friend to all and had excellent speaking skills.

You need to recognize your strengths, whatever they may be, and key in on them. Not everyone can be the star quarterback or the head cheerleader, but you can be important, nonetheless.

When he graduated from high school, Carnegie attended the local state teachers' college. His family was too poor to afford the one dollar a day it cost for room and board, so he continued to live at home while riding to and from school daily on horseback.

He wanted an education, and money was tight; but he made it work. From the early 1900's to the present day, college room and board has increased from one dollar a day to approximately sixty dollars a day or more; and that does not even include tuition and books. Even so, you, too, can find a way to get an education. OK, maybe you won't ride by horseback, but consider starting at the local community college to save money.

Carnegie did not, however, finish his work at the teachers' college; he left and went into theatre and acting. Not being able to make it in the entertainment industry, he became a salesman. But he was not happy in sales. One of his fondest memories was teaching public speaking at the teachers college. He quit his sales job and convinced the director of the local YMCA to let him teach a public speaking course. He ran into trouble during the very first class!

What worked well in college and drama school wasn't going over well with his students, who were mostly businessmen who wanted to improve their speaking ability. In desperation, he called on one of his students to make an impromptu speech. An impromptu speech is a five to eight minute speech with a characteristically short preparation time of only one to three minutes. This method of giving people experience in public speaking was to become a foundation of the Carnegie method. Carnegie training courses provide tools for effective public speaking by having participants think quickly to develop self-confidence and to gain experience so they can overcome the fear of speaking. This one-man class, based on impromptu speaking, would go on to become a multi-million dollar organization.

So, his success was simply by chance. He was failing at his public-speaking teaching job, so he improvised. And it worked! What can you learn from failure? You can learn to adapt, to make changes; and then to turn failure into achievement! Instead of being afraid of failure or viewing it as something to be avoided, turn it into a "stepping-stone" on the path to something wonderful. As long as you have a goal, look at success as the destination to achieving that goal and possible failure as an obstacle.

Carnegie had varied experiences, but he used them all in his lucrative career. You never know what work or volunteer experiences you may have that can later be valuable to you in the future. It's important to get that experience, nonetheless.

If your desire is to be effective in business or sales, then consider taking a Dale Carnegie course. While most don't intend to become public speakers, the fact is every time you talk you are publicly speaking, unless, of course, you're talking to yourself! Every time you talk with someone new, you will make a first impression; and you only have one chance to make a good first impression.

Now, let's talk about friends. Carnegie said, "You can make more friends in two months by becoming interested in other people than you can in two years by trying to get other people interested in you." Why is it that some teenagers are naturally popular while others are tremendously shy? If you are shy, then try the easiest of the six rules—smile. People who frequently smile are perceived to be more in control, at ease, and attractive than those who don't smile. How you are perceived is often what you will become!

Many young people avoid the spotlight and may feel anxious about participating in activities or making new friends. So, this is what you need to do. Fold your arms, naturally; it feels comfortable, doesn't it? Now fold your arms with the opposite arm on top. You had to think about it, didn't you? It's uncomfortable at first to do something in a different way, but you can get used to it if you try. Keep that in the back of your mind the next time you have to go out of your comfort zone.

Even though teenagers do want lots of friends, be aware of the influence they may have on you. Do they really have your best interests at heart or do they have selfish desires? Your parents know the great person that you are. They may not be worried about you; it may be your friends that cause them concern.

Studies show that there are differences in brain activity when adolescents are alone versus with their friends. The findings suggest that teenage peer pressure has a distinct effect on brain signals involving risk and reward, helping to explain why young people are more likely to misbehave and take risks when their friends are watching.[8]

OK, so now you know there's a reason for why you think differently with your friends! It's your brain signals, but don't try to give that excuse to your parents. Use the knowledge that your thinking process is different when friends are around to make smarter decisions.

The type of friends you have has a big impact on your life and who you are. The choices that you make are greatly influenced by the people closest to you. You need to think about who you hang around with and what activities result from spending time with those people. And if those activities aren't helping you become a better version of yourself, then you need to reconsider what's more important. If you decide that it is time to change your group of friends, have the guts to step forward and do so. You may think your high school friends will be friends for life; but the truth is you may have outgrown them and it's time for a change.

After all, life is really all about change. Circumstances change, and at times, your life will change. Some of these changes will be for the good; others may be devastating. Have the courage to make a change if it is in your best interest. In order to make a change, you have to be willing to take a chance; and then to take a chance is to risk. But make sure the risks you are taking are beneficial or good risks, such as taking a chance on being a class or club president.

8   Parker-Pope, Tara. "Teenagers, Friends and Bad Decisions". *New York Times Blog.* http://well.blogs.nytimes.com/2011/02/03/teenagers-friends-and-bad-decisions/

Many risks teenagers take have tremendous consequences. These include driving while intoxicated, experimenting with drugs, and being promiscuous. Even a one-minute risk can change your life forever.

What is risk anyway? Simply put, risk is a response to the unknown, taken in order to produce discovery and yield a gain. If a risk does not feel right to you, then it may be a dangerous risk. You must look at the longer-term consequences of risks. Be careful. Before you attempt a risk, go inside yourself and get a sense of how you really feel about it. If your head tells you it's silly or dangerous or too risky, but your friends insist that you try it, STOP. Think it through one more time.

Dale Carnegie also said, "Take a chance! All of life is a chance. The man who goes furthest is generally the one who is willing to do and dare. The 'sure thing' boat never gets far from shore." But also remember that you cannot row a boat in two directions at the same time! To be successful in the future, you'll have to take some risks, just make sure those risks are leading you in the right direction.

"*Take a chance. All of life is a chance. The man who goes furthest is generally the one who is willing to do and dare.*"

CHAPTER 7

Goals

"Give me a stock clerk with a goal and I'll give you a man who will make history. Give me a man with no goals and I'll give you a stock clerk."

—J C Penney

Think back several years to a time when you were about eight years old. At that age, would you have been able to practically support yourself, buy your own food, and purchase your own clothing? Probably not, but that's exactly what James Cash Penney had to do at such an early age. Young Penney worked on farms, raised pigs, traded horses, and grew watermelons to help support his family.

In 1895, two years after his high school graduation, Penney discovered what would prove to be his life's calling when he began working part-time as a sales clerk at a general store in Hamilton, Missouri. He worked extremely hard and proved himself so adept at merchandising that he advanced rapidly. Although his first year's salary was only twenty five dollars, by 1897 he was making three hundred a year, and his future appeared bright. Then he was given shattering news; his family doctor diagnosed Penney's recurring health problems as the early stages of tuberculosis, and told him that unless he moved to a dryer climate, he would likely die.

So he went west to Colorado, where he bought a butcher shop. That business failed, however, reportedly because Penney refused to furnish free liquor to the chef of the local hotel— his largest client. Penney decided to return to the retail business, taking temporary employment as a store clerk. Early in 1899, the owners of that business offered Penney a permanent clerkship in their Evanston, Wyoming, store at a monthly salary of fifty dollars. He readily accepted. He did so well that a few years later, when he was twenty six, the owners offered to make him a partner in a new store they planned to open in 1902. Penney persuaded them to open the store in a small mining town in Utah instead of the bigger city they had considered. Using his five hundred dollars savings and borrowing the rest of the two thousand necessary to become a one-third partner in the venture, Penney was back in business.

Penney called his store the "Golden Rule," because his idea was "to make money and build business through serving the community with fair and honest value."[9] Penney increased his profits each year, and five years later he bought out the other owners and became sole owner of the store. In the same year he purchased two additional stores in Wyoming.

---

9   Penney, J.C. *Fifty Years with the Golden Rule.* New York: Harper & Brothers, Publishers, 1950, 55.

Several things made Penney's success possible. His stores were all located in small communities where land costs were cheaper. He did not pay for elaborate fixtures and displays. He conducted business on a cash-only basis, and he treated his employees well. Perhaps most importantly, he carried merchandise that his customers wanted, ensuring a rapid inventory turnover. When one of his store managers had saved enough money, Penney would help him open a new store as part owner. The manager was responsible for investing one-third the amount necessary and Penney provided the remaining two-thirds. The manager would then have to agree to train someone to take his place at the existing store. In turn, new managers would train others until they started up their own stores as one-third partners. This arrangement allowed for rapid expansion in the early years of the business.

Between 1920 and 1930, more than 1,250 new stores opened, most of them on Main Streets in small towns across America. Even the Great Depression did little to halt the Penney expansion program. By 1932, the number of stores had increased to 1,473. When the business celebrated its 90th anniversary in 1992, twenty one years after Penney's death, it had become a firm surpassing $15 billion in annual sales, and employing approximately 190,000 associates.

Was it even possible for a poor country-boy Missouri farmer to own a multi-billion dollar retail store? James Cash Penney thought so. What about another boy from the mid-west who started his own company and became one of the richest men in the United States? That's right; Sam Walton started Wal-Mart in a small country town. But before he did, Walton joined J. C. Penney as a management trainee in Des Moines, Iowa, three days after graduating from college. This position paid him $75 a month.

Then came World War II and Walton served in the military. After leaving the military, he took his savings and also obtained a loan from his father to purchase a Ben Franklin variety store in Arkansas. J. C.

Penney and Sam Walton even met at a store. Penney showed Walton how to wrap packages using less paper and string.

J. C. Penney said, *"Give me a stock clerk with a goal and I'll give you a man who will make history. Give me a man with no goals and I'll give you a stock clerk."* With goal-setting, you, too, can have the tools to make your dreams come true. But first you must define your goals. I'm sure both Penney and Walton knew at an early age that they wanted to own their own company one day. With their lofty goals set, they put a plan of action into motion.

You'll notice that both these men had early retail experience. If you have a specific career in mind, then get job experiences working in that field. It's a great way to get a sense of the occupation. If your goal is to become a doctor or nurse, then find a part-time job at a doctor's office or at the hospital. Maybe you haven't a clue as to a career; work experience is a great way to sample career options.

Keep in mind that it will be necessary to set both short-term and long-term goals. A long-term goal may require a college degree and even advanced degrees. However, to achieve this, teenagers have to set objectives that will lead to the bigger dream. These objectives may require the short-term goal of improving your grades right now, for example. Don't worry, you have time. You can take little steps now in order to be able to achieve your ultimate goal in the future.

Choose goals that you have the power to reach, but ones that also require effort on your part. When you reach your goal, you want to feel a sense of accomplishment. Also, try to connect your goals with your values, interests, and talents. Be realistic but also optimistic.

So let's go over the steps. First, define your goal. While defining what it is you ultimately yearn for, ask yourself these questions: What do I want out of life? What do I most enjoy doing? What gives me joy? What do I value? Where do I see myself in ten, fifteen, or twenty years?

The next step after defining your goal is to research the steps necessary to achieve that goal. It would help to discuss those steps with a parent, grandparent, or school counselor. During that discussion, consider the possible roadblocks to accomplishing the goal and how to deal with them. If you think financial problems would get in the way, then also research scholarships.

Finally, set deadlines, especially if you are a procrastinator. If your goal involves continuing your education, then you will have deadlines for grade improvement, college admissions, and scholarship applications. About deadlines, make sure they are attainable and realistic. You want to present yourself with a challenge but not set yourself up for failure.

Consider something else about J. C. Penney's story. His first business venture, a butcher shop, depended on purchases by a local hotel. A man of high moral values, the straitlaced Penney refused to give liquor to the hotel cook in return for his trade. The butcher shop thus failed. He didn't comprise his values. Success was important to him, but not so important that he would do something which he felt was wrong.

Think of the values you hold that you would never compromise, even if it meant financial success. Never compromise on your self-respect, integrity, loyalty, personal safety, beliefs, or honesty. Because once lost, all the money in the world can never replace them!

Treat people the way you would like for them to treat you.

CHAPTER 8

Honesty

"Honesty is the first chapter in the book of wisdom."
—Thomas Jefferson

Thomas Jefferson, with help from John Adams and Benjamin Franklin, took on the task of writing a Declaration of Independence. This document, of course, stated that the colonies considered that they were free from British rule and were willing to fight for that freedom. This national treasure begins with, "We hold these truths to be self-evident that all men are created equal; that they are endowed by their creator with certain unalienable rights; that among these are life, liberty, and the pursuit of happiness."

Thomas Jefferson took seventeen days to write the Declaration of Independence, and the Second Continental Congress spent two days making some changes to the document. On July 4th, 1776, the Congress voted to accept this Declaration. Fifty years to the day, on July 4, 1826, the 90-year old 2nd President John Adams and 83-year-old 3rd President Jefferson died just hours apart.

We have all studied the works of Thomas Jefferson; but what you may not know about him is that despite his skills at writing and conversation, Jefferson was never a competent public speaker. When he had to speak publicly, he frequently mumbled and spoke in an inaudible voice that made it very difficult for people to hear him. His speeches were brilliantly written; he just wasn't able to deliver them in front of crowds!

His fear of public speaking made him an incredibly private president who tried to avoid the spotlight. For this reason, he started the tradition of sending the State of the Union message to Congress in writing so he would not have to present it. This tradition was followed until 1913 when it was broken by Woodrow Wilson.

Many young children dream of being president of the United States one day. To most, that would seem to be the ultimate goal. But Jefferson did not view the presidency as one of his major accomplishments! He wrote his own epitaph for his tombstone, and this is what he wanted as testimonials that he lived, and is by what he wished most to be remembered:

Here was buried
Thomas Jefferson
Author of the Declaration of American Independence
of the Statute of Virginia for religious freedom
& Father of the University of Virginia

Renowned American statesman Daniel Webster delivered a eulogy for these two great Americans. He encouraged the crowd to honor the liberty granted to them by Adams and Jefferson, saying, "let us cherish a strong affection for it, and resolve to maintain and perpetuate it."

Do you have a strong affection for our great nation? Are you willing to do your part to maintain and perpetuate our liberty? Never forget how the colonists and those in the military since then have fought dearly for it. One simple way you can do this as you turn eighteen is to vote. Before doing so, take time to research the candidates so that you can make an informed choice. Read all you can about the candidates and watch presidential debates.

Our country is strong, but so was another great government! Consider the fall of the Roman Empire. Back then the powerful, wealthy Roman Emperor had unyielding power. There's an old saying that goes "power corrupts and absolute power corrupts absolutely." The Emperor wanted power and control over the people. Cheap slave labor resulted in the unemployment of the people of Rome, who became dependant on hand-outs from the state. Unemployment was so bad that the government then subsidized the working class Romans, who didn't mind living a life of ease while the government took care of their every need. Then the thousands of unemployed Romans became bored and this led to civil unrest and rioting in the streets. That's why the gladiator games started—the mob was bored and needed to be amused.

Roman leaders were too busy taking care of their citizens to think about foreign invasions, and they had fierce foreign enemies! Does all of this sound familiar? Is any of this happening in our country today? In 537 AD during a siege on Rome by the Goths, the aqueducts which supplied Rome with water were destroyed. The people of Rome could not survive without water and the population of Rome fell by 90%.

As an emerging responsible citizen, do what you can to insure that something similar to this does not happen in America. President John F. Kennedy once said, "Ask not what your country can do for you—ask what you can do for your country." What that means is that instead of letting the government take care of you, you must take care of yourself, and do what you can to preserve the liberty of this great nation. Since this country was founded, each generation of Americans has been summoned to fight for our preservation. Get involved in politics and speak your mind when you see an injustice. It is true that one person can cause change. One person can make a difference. The preservation of our country is the responsibility of all its citizens.

While we are on the subject of politics, have you ever thought about this: *if pros and cons are opposite, is congress the opposite of progress?* That's just a joke! Even so, it is sad that it may sometimes actually be true. Citizens can and should hold Congress accountable.

One of the wonderful things about living in the United States is that we can have a voice in how we are governed. To do so, you need to become your own advocate in Congress. Find out about laws being proposed. If you don't approve, then voice your concern. They want votes, so senators and representatives should listen to their constituents. But to be effective, you must communicate properly with them. Keep your comments brief, pertinent, and factual and include your subject in the first paragraph. You can call Senators' or Representative's office or email them. Get involved.

Now back to Jefferson: he was a highly intelligent man, a man of vision, and a silent man. You may think the successful ones are those not afraid to speak in front of groups, the popular kids so to speak. I doubt very seriously that Thomas Jefferson was popular in high school; yet with his eloquent words, he formulated the goals of our nation. But he could not speak those words in front of a group.

Jefferson cleverly wrote, "Honesty is the first chapter in the book of wisdom." The first chapter of a book sets the stage for what will follow. In it characters are developed. Just as the first chapter is vital to understanding the plot, the most important chapter of your life's book is the first chapter of honesty. If you skip the first chapter, the rest is meaningless. This means that honesty is not only necessary for wisdom, it is the very foundation of wisdom and a firm foundation will determine your future.

We often think of older people as being wise or having wisdom because they can draw upon their life experiences. So, think of yourself as a book. In the beginning chapters of your life, include honesty every chance you get. Middle chapters will be your other good character traits; closing will be examples of your life's wisdom. And so it is written!

With your thoughts and actions, you are composing chapters of your own life. Make sure that your first chapter provides examples of your honesty for it, along with integrity, will be your most valuable traits. It is more than just telling the truth. It's living the truth.

Honesty is a direct reflection of your inner character. Character plays a big role in where you go in your life; being honest is a characteristic that employers and college interviewers look for in candidates. Learning how to be more honest will help you keep a clear conscious and will improve your memory because once a lie is told you've got to remember what you said. If you later contradict, then you'll be caught.

Being truthful is one of the most important traits you should look for in a mate and in a leader. Trust is important; if someone lies to you, then it is difficult to trust them again. Honesty is not just in dealing with others, but also in how you speak to yourself. Being too hard on yourself is not being truthful as is thinking too highly of yourself.

In a survey of twenty thousand students on issues of character, lying, and cheating, the vast majority of the teens surveyed agreed that trust and honesty are essential to personal relationships. If it is so important, than why lie to your parents? In fact, if you want more freedoms, then *don't* lie because your parents need to feel they can trust you. You would be surprised at the times parents might have been lenient, understanding, or even forgiving. But the time you had to spend grounded at home? That was for lying.

Another quote attributed to Jefferson is, "In matters of style swim with the current; in matters of principle stand like a rock." Have you ever observed a creek where water and leaves are constantly flowing over the rocks that remain stationary? Think of your values as rocks—they will always be there when other things will come and go. So, when it comes to honesty, stand like a rock. If you want to follow the latest styles and popular music, by all means go ahead. Everyone wants to be stylish as far as fashion is concerned. But never do the same with your values. Stand firm in your principles.

"Honesty is the first chapter in the book of wisdom"

CHAPTER 9

Intuition

"Intuition will tell the thinking mind where to look next."
—Jonas Salk

Jonas Salk was a doctor by trade and had no formal training as a virologist or as an immunologist. But without his intuition, a vaccination against the debilitating disease of polio may have been much delayed. At the height of the polio epidemic, in the 1940's and 1950's, most scientists believed that effective vaccines could only be developed with live viruses. Salk developed a "killed-virus" vaccine by growing a sample of the virus and then deactivating them by adding formaldehyde so that they could no longer reproduce. This would then be injected into the bloodstream, tricking the immune system into manufacturing protective antibodies.

Many researchers such as Polish-born virologist Albert Sabin, who was himself developing an oral "live-virus" polio vaccine, disagreed with Salk's approach. The March of Dimes, growing impatient with the time-consuming process of developing a "live-virus" polio vaccine, chose Salk for their researcher and put their resources behind him.

Jonas Salk, even as a child, spent a good deal of time thinking. Although not an avid reader, he did remember reading a book called *The Island Within* by Ludwig Lewisohn. Written even before Hitler and the Holocaust, it is about the social and psychological struggles of a Jewish family. This book resonated with Salk because he also had struggles within his own mind while he tried to figure out the world around him. Then during his career, he tried to understand how viruses work, how viruses think, and how the immune system works. Because of the way his mind worked, he was a living island within himself.

He pretended to be a virus so that he could understand it. That's one way of putting yourself in someone else's shoes. Try that the next time you're trying to figure something out. If there is a dispute, then put yourself in their shoes by stepping back and looking at the situation from the other person's point of view. Who knows, you too may have a revelation.

Jonas Salk told the story that during his second year in medical school, a professor one particular day told the class that it was possible to immunize against diphtheria and tetanus by the use of chemically-treated toxins. The very next day, they were told that for immunization against a virus disease, you have to experience the infection—that you could not induce immunity with inactivated, chemically-treated virus preparation.

Salk was struck by this contradiction. His intuition told him that both statements couldn't be true. He asked why this was so, and the answer that was given was in a sense, "because." There was no reasonable answer. Salk was not willing to agree with that explanation or lack thereof. And it's a good thing he didn't! Being intrigued is what motivated him.

Salk questioned the logic of the two contradictory statements. He trusted his inner voice. When asked about the eye-opener he had during that year in medical school, Salk said, "It's important to recognize that sometimes at a turning point, what's important is to let go of the way you were going, or the way you are going, to explore a new direction."[10]

Now think about that statement. Are you willing to let go of things and explore a new direction? There are times when that is exactly what is necessary. If things aren't working out the way you planned, then maybe it's time to make some adjustments. We are all too quick to simply accept the status quo without changing our way of thinking.

Intuition is a feeling, and we do not know the source of that impression. Some may call it a gut feeling or a hunch. In other words, intuition is that voice inside your head. I'm sure you've heard it when your friends tell you to go ahead and do something you feel is wrong. Your intuition is trying to protect you. Let it!

Perhaps you're stuck between two choices due to test anxiety or a poorly worded test question. If you studied for the test, your unconscious mind may prompt you toward the right answer even though you don't remember learning it. For that reason, your first instinct is often the correct answer. That is your subconscious intuition working.

Intuition can even be an essential decision-making tool. You've seen people who seem to know exactly what to do in any given circumstance. They can recognize the best option or course of action in even difficult situations. The solution just comes to them from somewhere in their subconscious mind. In emergencies, you often have to act on instinct or intuition; you don't have time to look it up on the World Wide Web.

10   Academy of Achievement. "Jonas Salk Interview." http://www.achievement.org/autodoc/page/sal0int-1

Intuition is our brain retrieving information from our subconscious mind. It is often a nagging feeling we can't quite put into words but you don't want to dismiss it either. Pay attention to it, it might be trying to tell you something. In Federal Bureau of Investigation (FBI) training, intuition is recognized as a characteristic and skill important to investigations.

Your intuition comes from within and it represents your values. So, when faced with a difficult situation, pause and check in with yourself to determine how you really feel about the situation. Ask yourself, "What's the right thing for me to do?" "What feels right?" Pay attention to uncomfortable feelings you may have because it may be an indication of something unsafe. Train yourself to trust your instinct because intuition goes further than just using common sense. It is something we can rely upon to make decisions that goes above and beyond our intelligent thinking.

Intuition will tell the thinking mind where to look next.

CHAPTER 10

Jobs

"Nothing is particularly hard if you divide it into small jobs."

—Henry Ford

enry Ford's father was a farmer in Dearborn, Michigan. He encouraged Henry's interest in the use of machines that were used on the farm. Steam-powered tractors fascinated the teenage Ford. They made him think about the way things work.

Two events dramatically changed Henry Ford's life. First, he received a watch for his 12th birthday. Second, for the first time he saw a horseless farm machine—a road engine used for driving threshing machines. One year later, using crude tools, he was able to put together a watch. Shortly thereafter, he built a working model of the road engine that had occupied his dreams.[11]

At sixteen, Ford left home for the nearby city of Detroit, where he found apprentice work as a machinist. After three years, he returned to Dearborn to work on the family farm, but continued to moonlight as a steam engine repairman. Several years later, he and his wife returned to Detroit, where Ford was hired as an engineer for the Edison Illuminating Company. Rising quickly through the ranks, he was promoted to chief engineer after just two years.

As chief engineer, he was on call twenty four hours a day, which made for irregular hours. But he used that to his advantage; he spent those hours on his efforts to build a gasoline-powered horseless carriage, or automobile. Ford tested the engine in his kitchen, with the engine clamped to the sink, the spark plug connected to the ceiling light socket, and the oil cup tended by his wife.

In 1896 he completed what he called the "Quadricycle," which consisted of a light metal frame fitted with four bicycle wheels and powered by a two-cylinder, four-horsepower gasoline engine.

Determined to improve upon what would later be called the automobile, Ford sold the quadricycle in order to continue building other vehicles. He received backing from various investors over the next seven years, some of whom formed the Detroit Automobile Company (later the Henry Ford Company) in 1899. His partners, eager to put a passenger car on the market, grew frustrated with Ford's constant attention to detail and his need to improve, and Ford left his namesake company in 1902. After his departure, that company was reorganized as the Cadillac Motor Car Company.

The following year, Ford established the Ford Motor Company; one month later, the first Ford car, the two-cylinder, eight-horsepower

11   History.com. "Personality: Henry Ford - January '97 World War II Feature" *History Net Where History Comes Alive World US History Online.* http://www. historynet.com/personality-henry-ford-january-97-world-war-ii-feature.htm

Model A, was assembled and built by hand from parts that were ordered from other companies. Models named A thru S would be produced in the following five years. All the while, Ford paid attention to detail. The following excerpt from his biography provides an example of that detail:

"I designed eight models in all before "Model T." They were: "Model A," "Model B," Model C," "Model F," "Model N," "Model R," "Model S," and "Model K." Of these, Models "A," "C," and "F" had two-cylinder opposed horizontal motors. In "Model A" the motor was at the rear of the driver's seat. In all of the other models it was under the hood at the front. Models "B," "N," "R," and "S" had motors of the four-cylinder vertical type. "Model K" had six cylinders. "Model A" developed eight horsepower. "Model B" developed twenty-four horsepower with a 4 ½-inch cylinder and a 5-inch stroke. The highest horsepower was in "Model K," the six-cylinder car, which developed forty horsepower. The largest cylinders were those of "Model "N," "R," and "S" which were 3 ¾ inches in diameter with a 3 3/8-inch stroke. "Model T" has a 3 ¾-inch cylinder with a 4-inch stroke. The ignition was by dry batteries in all excepting "Model B," which had storage batteries, and in "Model K" which had both a battery and magneto. In the present model, the magneto is a part of the power plant and is built in. The clutch in the first four models was of the cone type; in the last four and in the present model, of the multiple disc type. The transmission in all the cars has been planetary. "Model A" had a chain drive. "Model B" had a shaft drive. The next two models had chain drives. Model A" had a 72-inch wheel base. Model "B," which was an extremely good car, had 92 inches. "Model K" had 120 inches. "Model C" had 78 inches. The others had 84 inches, and the present car has 100 inches. ...Model "A" weighed

1,250 pounds. The lightest cars were Models "N" and "R"; they weighed 1,050 pounds, but they were both runabouts. The heaviest car was the six-cylinder, which weighed 2,000 pounds. The present car weighs 1,200 pounds. (Note: That was in 1922, now they're almost 4,000 pounds.)"[12]

The Model T, also known as the "Tin Lizzie," made its debut in 1908 and was an immediate success. Ford soon had more orders than the company could satisfy. As a result, he put into practice techniques of mass production that would revolutionize American industry, including the use of large production plants, standardized, interchangeable parts; and the moving assembly line. Mass production significantly cut down on the time required to produce an automobile, which allowed costs to stay low. In 1914 Ford also increased the daily wage for an eight-hour day for his workers to $5 (up from $2.34 for nine hours), setting a standard for the industry.

The original price of $850 for a Model T was still too high for many customers. To lower the price, Ford found ways to reduce production costs. His system helped reduce the assembly time of a Ford automobile from about twelve and one half worker hours in 1912 to about one and one-half worker hours in 1914.

As the company's production costs fell, Ford passed much of the savings on to his customers. The price of a Model T dropped to $550 in 1913, $440 in 1915, and $290 in 1925, putting the automobile within reach of the average family.

Henry Ford did not invent the automobile, or the gas engine, or the assembly line. His contribution was in perfecting each. Leonardo da Vinci had even sketched a horseless, mechanized cart as early as the 1500's. The moving assembly line had already transformed the meatpacking industry; Ford's success was making it work for complex

---

12   Ford, Henry. [p.69-71, *My Life and Work*, 1922]

manufacturing. He once said, "If I could save every one of my workers fifty steps per day, then I'd save miles by the end of the year."[13]

Even with the success of the Model T, salesmen wanted Ford to make changes and to manufacture more than one model at a time. Ford refused, and just made the Model T for the next nineteen years. But he did tell the salesmen that a customer could have the Model T painted any color he would like *as long as it was black*. He stuck to his principles and produced what he knew for sure would work.

Between 1913 and 1927, Ford factories produced more than 15 million Model Ts. The 10-gallon fuel tank was located under the front seat. Because gasoline was fed to the engine only by gravity, and also because the reverse gear offered more power than the forward gears, the Model T frequently had to be driven up a steep hill backward.[14]

As a side note, the Model T had about seven thousand parts and took about ninety minutes to put those parts together on the assembly line. A single car now has an average of thirty thousand parts, counting every part down to the smallest screws. It now takes twenty to thirty hours to put it all together. It is safe to say that Henry Ford's method in the early 1900's was efficient!

Henry Ford was a mastermind at mass production. Then world wars and the rise of labor unions, among other things, caused the company's finances to decline. His grandson, Henry Ford II, took over the company in 1945. Grandson Henry hired a team of expert managers and introduced new marketing methods and automobile designs. In the year 1949, after the reorganization, the company was again profitable.

So, that's how your shiny vehicle came into being. It is a tremendous responsibility to operate a thirty thousand part piece of machinery weighing about two tons. Keep that in mind the next time you get

---

13   New York Daily News. " Ford's assembly line turns 100: How it changed society" http://www.nydailynews.com/autos/ford-assembly-line-turns-100-changed-society-article-1.1478331

14   History.com. http://www.history.com/topics/model-t

behind the wheel. Taking your eyes off the road for just one second can cause you to drift out of your lane because your car goes where your eyes go. As a driver, you must insist that your passengers behave and not cause any problems while you are driving.

Henry Ford said, "Nothing is particularly hard if you divide it into small jobs." Each team member on the assembly line had his own job to do. Divided into small jobs, an automobile could be easily assembled because each employee turned the same wrench on the same type of bolt numerous times per day—even unskilled workers could learn it. They repeated the same process each day and became good at their jobs.

Just as the thought of assembling an automobile yourself can be daunting, so can the stress of a large school or work project. Follow the example of Ford and divide it into small jobs, and work on a small portion at a time, and don't waste any steps. Before you know it, you'll have that project assembled.

Part of the reason we get distracted when trying to work on big tasks *is* because they're so big. If you break them down into little pieces, they get easier to work with. Also, the longer you avoid something, the larger it seems to get—because you become more and more overwhelmed.

That's why, when sitting down to start a project, you instead check Instagram, or Facebook, or email—you're avoiding the big project. When breaking a project down into parts, do the easiest components first. Get that part out of the way. Then you will have a feeling of accomplishment, and the harder tasks will seem easier. Don't delay; start right away!

Library of Congress. Henry Ford and his first car.

CHAPTER 11

Kindness

"No kind action ever stops with itself. One kind action leads to another."

—Amelia Earhart

W hen ten-year-old Amelia Mary Earhart saw one of the Wright Brothers' first airplanes at a state fair in 1908, she was not impressed. "It was a thing of rusty wire and wood and looked not at all interesting," she dismissively said.[15] It was only almost a decade later when she attended a stunt-flying exhibition, that she became seriously interested in aviation. A pilot spotted her and

---

15   "The Official Website of Amelia Earhart" http://www.ameliaearhart.com/about/
bio.html

a friend and swooped down close to them. That's when she knew she had to fly.

By then she had graduated from high school, and like most, she wasn't sure what she wanted her occupation to be. She dropped out of college to become a nurse's aide tending wounded soldiers from World War I. Then she studied to become a mechanic, but soon was back in school studying for a career in medicine. She had decided to go into medical research. That is, until she took her first plane ride.

In 1928 Earhart was invited on a historic flight across the Atlantic. Together with two other pilots, both of whom were male, she flew across the Atlantic Ocean serving as trip navigator. After twenty one hours in the air, the plane landed in Wales. She was the first woman to make the flight across the Atlantic.

She was hailed back in the United States as a hero and was even invited to the White House to meet President Calvin Coolidge. She was not, however, satisfied. Her desire was to make the same trip across the Atlantic, but this time she wanted to pilot the plane *and* navigate by herself. On May 20, 1932, she took off from Newfoundland aboard a bright red single engine Lockheed Vega airplane. Her destination was Paris, France.

Due to bad weather, she had to cut the flight short and land in Ireland. Up to then, Charles Lindbergh had been the only person to fly across the Atlantic solo. She continued to fly and broke many records.

She still wasn't satisfied and wanted to become the first woman to fly around the world. In June 1937, she and her navigator took off from Miami, Florida. They got all the way across Africa and Asia to New Guinea in the South Pacific. That was the last place they were seen. She, her navigator, and her plane were never found.

Earhart's convictions were strong, and this tomboy was no stranger to criticism, doubts, and disapproval. She was determined she would be in anything other than a traditional female role and even kept a scrapbook of newspaper clippings about successful women in predominantly male-oriented fields.

Just as one triumph in her life led to another and then another, the quote attributed to her is just as true. She said, "No kind action ever stops with itself. One kind action leads to another." Earhart went on to say, "A single act of kindness throws out roots in all directions, and the roots spring up and make new trees. The greatest work that kindness does to others is that it makes them kind themselves."

Kindness begets kindness. It's like a chain reaction along the lines of "as you sow, so shall you reap." If you give kindness, you will get kindness in return. Have you ever seen someone yawn and then you feel impelled (forced) to yawn or heard someone laugh, and then you in turn start laughing? It's the same principle.

You cannot pass a day that is not loaded with opportunities to practice thoughtfulness. By truly listening to others, being patient, helping, and saying thanks, you are showing consideration for others. And more frequently than not, they will return it. We never know how far an act of kindness can go.

Using the words of Earhart, no action ever stops with itself, one thing leads to another. So start a smile chain. It is often said that a smile is contagious. A warm, friendly smile can go a long way because it is an expression of a positive attitude that can then be passed on to others. If you smile at someone, they will no doubt smile back. Practice it sometime. Look for the saddest person you can find, and then smile at that person. You will notice a change in his disposition that may very well affect the rest of his day. Then that will affect those he comes in contact with.

Besides, smiling is good for your health and well-being. It reduces stress that your body and mind feel and helps to generate positive emotions. Once the smiling muscles in our face begin to work, there's a signal going to the brain that causes an increase in our feeling of joy.

That's why we often feel happier around children—they smile more. Children smile an average of four hundred times per day, while happy adults smile forty to fifty times per day. How many times a day do you smile? Go ahead and keep track!

"A single act of kindness throws out roots in all directions,
and the roots spring up and make new trees."

CHAPTER 12

Leadership

"The greatest leader is not necessarily the one who does the greatest things. He is the one that gets the people to do the greatest things."

—Ronald Reagan

Ronald Reagan was an actor, governor of California, and the 40th President of the United States, becoming the first actor to serve in that role. He was born in a working-class family in Illinois; they moved a lot throughout his childhood.

Reagan faced challenges of various degrees throughout his career—including a heartbreaking divorce, the loss of his Warner Brothers acting contract, and his unsuccessful bid for the GOP presidential nomination in 1976. But he never stopped pursuing his dream, says Margot Morrell in her new book *Reagan's Journey: Lessons from a Remarkable Career.*[16]

The summer after high school graduation, he drove his girlfriend to a college ninety miles away for registration. He went straight to the college president's office. In his talk with the president, Reagan asked for assistance in the form of a scholarship for needy students. The college granted Reagan an athletic scholarship and also provided an on-campus job in the dining hall for Reagan so he could afford to eat as well as attend classes.

Now picture that. A president of the most powerful nation on Earth, born on the second floor of an old apartment building, did not have the money to attend college and had to ask for a handout. What's more, he washed dishes so that he could eat. Being a skilled athlete and being willing to work a menial job put him on the road to the presidency. He was probably afraid to approach the college president for help, but he did it nonetheless.

Reagan started his career as a lifeguard and a sportscaster. This future president saved an estimated seventy seven lives in his summers as a lifeguard. A lifeguard is often looked up to by swimmers and is seen as an authority figure or a leader.

If you like to be outdoors, you should consider becoming a Red Cross certified lifeguard. You must be at least fifteen years old, take a swimming course, attend training to learn how to prevent and respond to emergencies, know CPR skills, and pass a test. One of the most popular benefits is getting to enjoy the sun and fun while getting paid for it! Being a lifeguard will also help you develop leadership skills you can use later in life.

---

16   Morrell, Margot. *Reagan's Journey; Lessons From a Remarkable Career.* New York: Simon Schuster. May 3, 2011.

Ronald Reagan had the reputation as a strong leader. That's why on January 20, 1981, Iran released fifty-two Americans who had been held hostage for 444 days, minutes after the presidency had passed from Jimmy Carter to Reagan. The hostages were placed on a plane in Tehran as Reagan delivered his inaugural address.

The Iran Hostage Crisis had begun in November of 1979, when a group of several hundred militant Islamic students broke into the United States embassy in Tehran and took its occupants hostage. The students initially intended to hold the hostages for only a short time, but changed their plans when their act received widespread praise in Iran. In response, President Carter imposed economic sanctions but nothing worked until Reagan took over the reins. You see, Iran knew that Reagan was going to be a strong leader in the world.

In 1961, the communist leaders built a wall separating East Germany from West Germany. The purpose was to keep Westerners from entering East Germany and undermining the Socialist state and also to keep East Germans from defecting to freedom. Reagan stood in front of that wall in 1987, when he publicly called on Soviet General Secretary Mikhail Gorbachev to "open this gate. . . and tear down this wall?"

Reagan's public speech and prodding in private meetings with Gorbachev paid off. When the Soviet Union failed to send troops to stand down the East German protesters, they essentially gave the green light for change. East Germany's leader stepped down, and a new leader emerged. On November 9, 1989, the order came and the political wall came down. Talk about Reagan's power of persuasion!

The Heritage Foundation states, "There is one Western leader above all others who forced the Soviets to give up the Brezhnev Doctrine and abandon the arms race, who brought down the Berlin Wall, and who ended the Cold War at the bargaining table and not on the battlefield.

The one leader responsible, more than any other, for leading the West to victory in the Cold War is President Ronald Reagan."[17]

Reagan was known as the Great Communicator; his experience working as a sportscaster no doubt helped hone his communication skills. His approach was always simple, clear, direct and caring; and he was able to connect with seemingly everyone from the common man to veteran politicians—a powerful skill in Washington D.C. and beyond. Even when Reagan disagreed with his political opponents, they report he wasn't disagreeable.

The fascinating thing about Reagan's legacy is that this poor kid from nowhere sets his sights on lofty goals, and was able to achieve each and every one of them. He entered college at a time when only seven percent of the population went to college, and he graduated in the midst of the Great Depression, when unemployment is at 24%. He had a way of making things work for his career. A Hollywood agent in the 1940's remembered Reagan as constantly working the phone, staying in touch with people, looking for opportunities, promoting his career.

You could do the same by being an advocate for yourself; be a self-promoter. A person can wait all day, all year, their entire lifetime for an opportunity to come to them while sitting on the living room couch. Or that person can get out into the world and look for opportunities.

Ronald Reagan said that the greatest leader is the one who gets the people to do the greatest things. In other words, the leader must have clear and definite goals and be able to communicate those goals to all. Leaders must first have a vision of what it is they want to accomplish. That is necessary in order to persuade others to follow them.

Leadership, the ability to guide a group, actually begins at any early age. It is said that one baby in a group of more than two babies always turns out to be a leader. The child who is a potential leader, is first, never

---

17   http://www.heritage.org/research/lecture/ronald-reagan-and-the-fall-of-communism

distracted in his thinking, and second, is creative. These same abilities, concentration and creativity, can be nurtured. If you're not a born leader, then you can work on these two areas to become one. And it helps tremendously to be likeable. Reagan was a likeable fellow. To become an effective leader you must start with yourself. Do what you can to refine your personal qualities and strengthen your character. Without being likeable and having personal integrity, nothing will work.

Another leadership lesson that can be learned from Reagan is not to micromanage. He had a unique way of listening to people and of taking their ideas into consideration while at the same time never losing sight of what it was he wanted to accomplish.

It was said that he often sat in on a meeting, just listening for the most part; and then would come in at the end, summarize what everyone had to say, and then put a plan on the table for all to consider. Now, that's a leader, he listened to others, made them feel like they were part of the problem-solving process, but ultimately the decision was Reagan's.

Leadership requires practice; and believe it or not, it is a skill that can be learned. If you want to be a leader, you have to learn to speak like a leader. And you have to speak with confidence. Reagan surely did. This great president once said, "America is too great for small dreams." He set high goals, even as high as dismantling the evil empire of communism, and through his leadership style and communication skills, he achieved them all. Leaders dream big.

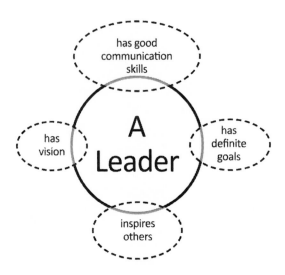

"The greatest leader is not necessarily the one who does the greatest things. He is the one that gets the people to do the greatest things."

CHAPTER 13

Money Management

"A penny saved is a penny earned."
—Benjamin Franklin

Ben Franklin was a man of many and varied accomplishments. He was a writer, scientist, musician, inventor, and innovator, despite only receiving two years of formal schooling. His ideas and principles helped shape our great nation.

Poor Ben was the victim of sibling rivalry. He was one of seventeen children. How would you like to try to get along with sixteen brothers and sisters? Some of his older brothers were role models; they were in the print shop business, and Ben wanted to do the same. The problem was his older brothers couldn't be bothered with Ben.

When he was twelve, his father sent him to work as an apprentice in a print shop run by an older brother. The young Franklin immediately took to the trade of printing, but his brother repeatedly refused to publish any of his writings. Not to worry.

Franklin fought back by writing letters under a pseudonym to his brother's newspaper. He pretended to be "Mrs. Silence Dogood," supposedly a middle-aged widow; and this fictitious figure became immensely popular with the readers. Because of wit and humor, Mrs. Dogood even received several marriage proposals. When Franklin's cover was blown, his big brother was not amused.

A disagreement ensued and the two parted ways. But all was not lost because Franklin was determined to be successful in the printing business. Printing is an industry with high equipment costs, so Franklin needed support to get set up on his own. His honesty and ambition won him the confidence of friends with the money necessary to start a print shop. Then his diligence and work ethic made the business a success. In his autobiography, Franklin noted that he often worked past 11 p.m. to get a job done, and that if necessary, he would stay overnight to redo it. In a town the size of Philadelphia, people quickly noticed this extra effort, and Franklin's growing reputation lured customers away from his rivals.

By far the largest part of Franklin's business was his newspaper and his almanacs, but he also did government printing. From 1730 on Franklin was the printer of all the money issued by Pennsylvania, New Jersey, and Delaware.

Beginning in 1929, Franklin's face would grace the front of the $100 bill. Many people refer to one hundred bills as Franklins. A newly designed $100 made its debut in 2013. Ben's picture is still on the front, twice. If you ever get your hands on one, hold it up to a light and you can see a faint image of Franklin in the blank space to the right of the portrait.

Franklin was terrified of debt. His view was that through the acquisition of debt, man essentially sold his own independence. He believed that a person could not be free if they were straddled with debt; that it was a force that pulled a person down. He would be astonished to learn how many Franklins are now due and payable for our current national debt!

According to a survey of 1,000 renters by Rent.com, more than three quarters of people between the ages of 18 and 24 spend more than they earn each month. Since they haven't established good credit yet, it's safe to say they are paying high interest rates on their resulting credit card balance.[18] Many rely on credit cards to make it to the next payday.

This type of credit card debt is not sustainable. Paying only a small amount on the credit card statement each month means that it will take a long, long time to pay it off. The longer it takes to pay it back, the more it will cost in the long run because interest is charged. That means that it may take ten years to pay off that pizza that was charged to a credit card. Wouldn't it be better to instead have a peanut butter and jelly sandwich you can afford?

You've heard of successful athletes, for example, who've made millions of dollars and then ended up broke. How could that happen, you may wonder? To put it simply, they had bad spending habits. They did not understand the difference between needs and wants. And people who don't understand this difference usually struggle with financial problems for the rest of their lives.

A need is something that is necessary in your life, like food or shelter. On the other hand, a want is something that is not necessary in your life but rather something you would like to have. Don't misunderstand, wants can be extremely motivating—they can push you to accomplish

---

18   White, Martha C. "Today's Young Adults Will Never Pay Off Their Credit Card Debts." *TIME Business*. http://business.time.com/2013/01/17/todays-young-adults-will-never-pay-off-their-credit-card-debts/

your goals. So the key is not to totally eliminate wants but to keep them under control until such a time as you can afford them. Sure you need reliable transportation, but can you really afford a brand new Lexus now?

Ben Franklin cleverly said, "A penny saved is a penny earned." The notion appears to have been that, by declining to spend a penny and to save one's money instead, you are a penny up rather than a penny down. And when you save money in a savings account it *earns* interest as opposed to spending money you don't have and having to *pay* interest. Properly saved or invested, your money can earn money.

Here's a question for you to consider: Would you rather have a penny doubled each day for thirty days or one million dollars? You can ponder that for a while. The majority of millionaires are self-made. Unless you're born with a silver spoon in your mouth, wealth will not happen by accident. It comes from a strategy of slow and steady investments.

OK, about the investment question, time's up! Did you choose the million dollars? Most people do. But let's analyze it. At the end of Day 5, you would have sixteen cents. With the increase being continually doubled each and every day, you would have $5.12 on Day 10, then $5,242.88 on Day 20. Get the picture? So what would it be on Day 30? Get out your calculator and figure it out.

This is called the power of compounding. A one hundred percent return every day (the process of being doubled) is extremely unlikely, but the principle holds true for smaller returns. You see, when you save or invest, your money earns interest, and then interest is earned on the interest.

Consider this example: A person saves two hundred dollars per year in an account earning ten percent interest. At the end of ten years, he would have over $3,500 by saving only $200 per year. The secret is to start early and not touch the savings for a long time because the largest growth comes at the very end.

So get out that piggy bank, dust it off, and start saving! By the way, the origin of piggy banks dates back nearly six hundred years in a time before real banks even existed. Then people commonly stored their money at home in common kitchen jars. During The Middle Ages, which lasted from the collapse of the Roman Empire to the 15th century, dishes and pots were made of economical orange-colored clay called pygg. Whenever folks could save an extra coin or two, they dropped it into one of their clay jars—a pygg pot.

*Don't let debt weigh you down. Be a good
money manager. If you can't afford it, don't buy it.*

CHAPTER 14

Networking

"This mode of instantaneous communication must inevitably become an instrument of immense power, to be wielded for good or for evil, as it shall be properly or improperly directed"

—Samuel Morse

Could you survive without your telephone? Can you imagine life before the telephone? How did people stay connected back then? Telegraph. Pony Express. Carrier Pigeon. Drumbeats. Smoke Signals.

A communication network is not new; Samuel Morse had visions of one as far back as the 1800's. He was born in Massachusetts and entered

Yale at the age of 14, earning money by painting portraits. He studied religious philosophy and mathematics, but his passion was art. Upon graduating from college, he sailed to England for more study in the arts.

When he returned to America, Morse got married and received commissions to paint portraits of former Presidents John Adams and James Monroe, and a series of works depicting the inner workings of the U.S. government to hang in the halls of Congress. But the pinnacle of his artist career was an offer in 1825 to paint Marquis de Lafayette who was one of the lead French supporters of the American Revolution. Morse had to be away from his home in Connecticut to travel to Washington D.C. to work on these commissioned projects.

While working in D. C., Morse received a letter from his father—delivered via the standard, slow-moving horse messengers of the day—that Morse's wife was gravely ill. He immediately left the Capitol and raced to his Connecticut home. By the time he arrived, however, his wife was not only dead—she had already been buried. It is believed that the grief-stricken Morse, devastated that it had taken days for him to receive the initial notification of his wife's illness, shifted his focus away from his art career and instead dedicated himself to improving the state of long-distance communication.

After his wife's death, Morse once again travelled to Europe, and on the return trip had a chance encounter with an American scientist who showed Morse his latest work on electromagnetism, inspiring Morse's idea of using electricity to transmit messages over long distances. You see, an innovative idea may begin as a mere thought in your head and then can be sparked by a person you meet who shares a piece of information with you that provides the missing link. Morse showed interest in another's work and ideas and was able to incorporate those ideas into his own invention. That is the value of networking with others.

Morse invented a single-circuit telegraph that worked by pushing the operator key down to complete the electric circuit of the battery.

This action sent the electric signal across a wire to a receiver at the other end. All the system needed was a key, a battery, wire and a line of poles between stations for the wire and a receiver.[19]

He then coauthored what became known as the Morse code. It assigned a set of dots (short marks) and dashes (long marks) to letters of the alphabet and numbers based on the frequency of use. Letters such as "E" got a simple code, while those used infrequently such as "Q" got a longer and more complex code. Initially, the code, when transmitted over the telegraph system, appeared as marks on a piece of paper that the telegraph operator would then translate back to into English. The operators got so good at their jobs that they were able to understand the code just by listening to the clicking of the receiver, so the paper was replaced by a receiver that created more pronounced beeping sounds.

You've heard of SOS, the internationally recognized distress signal. Contrary to popular belief, SOS does not stand for Save Our Ship. Instead, the letters were chosen because they are easy to transmit and interpret in Morse code. "S" is three dots, and "O" is three dashes.

Morse received a U. S. patent for the telegraph, but he needed funds and government support to go forward. He sought assistance from Congress for nearly six years before money was finally approved. He also had to obtain private funds to extend the telegraph lines. A telegraph cable was stretched from coast to coast and a transatlantic line was also placed between the United States and Europe.

Small telegraph companies began to pop up and trains started being dispatched by telegraph in 1851, the same year Western Union began business. The Postal Telegraph System also entered the field in 1881 and would merge with Western Union sixty years later.

Until 1877, all rapid long-distance communication depended upon the telegraph. That same year, a rival technology developed that would

---

19   http://www.history.com/topics/inventions/telegraph

again change the face of communication—the telephone. By 1879, patent litigation between Western Union and the infant telephone system was ended in an agreement that largely separated the two services.[20]

Western Union stayed in business even after the telephone was invented because they developed what was known as the telegram— messages in yellow envelopes hand-delivered by a courier. Years ago it was cheaper to send a telegram than to place a long-distance telephone call. Western Union delivered its last telegram in 2006. They now focus on money transfers and other financial services.

Prior to the telegraph, it took days, weeks, and even months for messages to be delivered from one location to another. After the transatlantic cable was in place, a message from London to New York City could be sent in mere minutes, and the world suddenly became smaller. Information and national news could now be shared. By the 1860's some even thought that it would make newspapers obsolete!

Samuel Morse even said, *"If the presence of electricity can be made visible in any part of the circuit, I see no reason why intelligence may not be transmitted instantaneously by electricity."* One hundred years after that statement, we have the Internet! Did he make a lot of money from inventing the telegraph and the Morse code? Well, only after he took his case all the way to the Supreme Court in a patent dispute.

Morse also said, *"This mode of instantaneous communication must inevitably become an instrument of immense power, to be wielded for good or for evil, as it shall be properly or improperly directed."* Over 150 years ago, he recognized that networks of communication have tremendous power that is both good and evil and that it may be improperly directed. Always remember that your system of communication is not private and that someone may use your information in evil ways.

---

20   Bellis, Mary. "The History of the Electric Telegraph." *About.Com.* http:// inventors.about.com/od/tstartinventions/a/telegraph.htm

So, how do you link up with your friends? Instagram. Facebook. Mark Zuckerberg's idea for Facebook started as a way for fellow Harvard students to connect with each other. He realized the importance of networking. A strong network will be critical to your professional survival. The professional person's version of Facebook is LinkedIn.

Start now developing your own personal, professional network. Begin by developing a list of everyone you know and identify how you know that person (friend, relative, classmate, neighbor, coworker, etc.). Your list can be in an Excel spreadsheet, a Word table, a spiral notebook, or an address book. Your phone contact list is a great way to start, but keep in mind you should expand on just phone numbers, also add e-mail and mailing addresses. Facebook and Instagram apps are great ways to stay in touch with people you know and to post important news, but you also need the list that includes other contact information.

And keep adding to your network. These groups of people will become valuable to you as you get older. Building a solid network is a continuous process. When you enter the world of work, you will no doubt receive business cards from associates. Save them, and on the back of each, write something memorable about the person who gave it to you. You never know when you may need a favor from that person.

Invest in knowing people. Don't be afraid to meet new people every chance you get. Go beyond just knowing their names, find out something about each member in your network. Remember their birthdays, for example; or send each a Christmas card. Call members of your network you have not seen in a while and make a lunch date.

If you haven't met many people yet, you may wonder what you would say to someone you just met. People like to talk about themselves, their jobs, and their families. So just start by asking a simple question. Then listen to their response to get your idea for your next question. Be interested in what they have to say.

The point is, you can learn from other people, especially adult role models. Don't be intimidated by people you find yourself in conversation with, even if they are your bosses or your senators. You must remember that even though a person may have a prestigious title, he is a normal person just like you. Besides, adults enjoy chatting with young people.

After a while, it will become easier and easier to meet strangers. That is not to say you should go up to all strangers and begin a conversation. By all means, be friendly, but use caution. Always have those feelers out to assess any possible dangers.

Social media can be a great tool to keep in touch with your network. But do not let it be your only means of communicating. Some of the negative effects associated with teens' social media use include cyber bullying and online harassment. These are serious offenses. If anyone is bothering you online or if they make you feel uncomfortable (remember your inner voice), report it to an adult immediately. Left unchecked, it will only become more dangerous.

As you build relationships, doors will open. Opportunities will become available. And never burn bridges! There may be a time when you need someone in your network. If it's a boss or coworker, then you may need to use him as a job reference. If it's a friend or family member, he may have leads for you to make your first big sale if you become a salesperson.

So never miss a chance to meet and make a new friend. And who knows? That friend may have a friend who has a cousin who has a brother, who has an aunt, who owns a company that might hire you someday. That is actually how it often works in the real world!

Develop a network of people

CHAPTER 15

Optimism

"A stumbling block to the pessimist is a stepping stone to the optimist."

—Eleanor Roosevelt

leanor Roosevelt, wife of 32nd President Franklin D. Roosevelt, struggled to overcome an unhappy childhood, betrayal in her marriage, and a controlling mother-in-law. Her life's goal was to improve the quality of life for others.

She was born as Anna Eleanor Roosevelt in 1884 to Elliott Roosevelt and Anna Hall Roosevelt. Her father, Elliott, was committed to an asylum in France when Eleanor was but a young child. It wasn't long until her uncle, Theodore Roosevelt, had his brother Elliott returned to the United States to seek treatment for his alcoholism and narcotic addiction. That same year, her mother died; two years later, her father died. So by the time Eleanor Roosevelt was ten years of age, she was an orphan. During her high school years she devoted her spare time to charity, often volunteering in the East Side slums of New York.

As a young woman, she was introduced to her father's fifth cousin, Franklin D. Roosevelt, a 20 year old young and brilliant Harvard University student. In 1903 soon after a White House reception and dinner with her uncle, President Theodore Roosevelt, the couple started seeing each other in secret. They even waited several months after becoming engaged to tell Franklin's mother, Sara Delano Roosevelt, because she opposed the couple's union.

In 1904, Eleanor and Franklin were married and settled into a home purchased by Franklin's mother. At first the gift seemed generous, but the gift had one condition attached: Franklin's mother would visit at any time. Then Eleanor Roosevelt's mother-in-law purchased the home next to the newlywed couple and had doors installed between the homes on every level, and eventually fired all of the household help and became the nanny to Eleanor's five children.

The Roosevelt family started spending their holidays at Campobello Island, New Brunswick, on the Maine–Canada border. While vacationing on the island in August 1921, Franklin was suddenly attacked by polio. This led to permanent paralysis of his legs. He would later found the March of Dimes to raise money for research into a cure for this paralytic illness. His disability was played down and care was taken to not have photographs taken of FDR in the wheelchair so that his paralysis could be concealed from the public.

Her husband's paralysis led Eleanor to replace him in many aspects of his work. She started making public appearances and worked in promoting a 48-hour work week, minimum wage, and the abolition of child labor. Her work in New York politics led to Franklin Roosevelt's nomination as candidate for governor and then president.

Franklin, or FDR as he was called, became President in March of 1933 at one of the worst points of the Great Depression. On the eve of his inauguration he inspired confidence with the people when he told them "The only thing we have to fear is fear itself." Roosevelt began by winning the confidence of ordinary Americans through regular "fireside chats" on the radio.

Not only in the United States, but many countries throughout the world were in debt after World War I. Millions of people were out of work and poverty rose. These conditions meant that countries were susceptible to the rise of Communism and Fascist dictatorships.

Fascist countries, Germany, Italy, and Japan, were known as the Axis. The Allies on the other hand were made up to a total of fifty countries, led by Great Britain, the Soviet Union, France, China, and the United States. They opposed the Axis.

Many Germans believed that only a strong leader could make their nation proud again. The Nazi Party rose to power in Germany, with Adolf Hitler as its leader because he was a powerful speaker and influenced many to follow him. His goal was to make Germany the most powerful country in the world. Hitler became a dictator with complete control; so powerful that he even killed those who opposed him.

But as a young boy, Hitler's most ardent goal was to become a priest. Later, he changed his mind and desired to become an artist. His dad would not allow young Hitler to even consider those choices. His father instead sent him to a strict school where Hitler rebelled. How would the world have been different if Hitler actually had the opportunity to become a priest or an artist?

Hitler started invading countries in Europe a few years after FDR's 1936 election for his second term. Roosevelt was focused on the problems at home but things in Europe were heating up. So, in order to prepare for war, two months before the 1940 election, the U. S. Congress passed the Selective Service Act. It called for the first peacetime draft in American history. To serve, men had to be five feet tall, weigh 105 pounds, have correctable vision, and at least half their teeth.

The Democratic Party then broke the 150-year old two-term tradition set by George Washington and nominated FDR for a third term in 1940. A lack of desire to change leadership amid crisis probably weighed heavily on the minds of voters. Roosevelt won 54.7 percent of the vote.

On December 7, 1941, at 7:55 am on a Sunday, hundreds of Japanese warplanes attacked the American Pacific fleet anchored at Pearl Harbor, Hawaii. Eight battleships were either sunk or damaged. One hundred-sixty-four American aircraft were destroyed, and 2,403 Americans were killed. On the day that President Roosevelt would call "a date which will live infamy," the Japanese also hit Guam, Wake Island, the Philippines, Malaya, and Hong Kong. The very next day, the United States declared war on Japan. Three days later Germany and Italy declared war on the United States.

With the war still going on in 1944, FDR was again elected president. This election was momentous, not only because it was his fourth term, but because he was seriously ill, and he and his aides carefully hid his failing health from the American people. FDR's four-term victory led to the passage in 1951 of the 22nd Amendment to the Constitution barring presidents from serving more than two full terms. The deception about his health helped pave the way for the now-familiar custom in which candidates must release results of their physicals and to disclose income tax returns.

Franklin D. Roosevelt died three months into his fourth term. Eleanor Roosevelt was a firm supporter of her husband in his political career but their marriage became platonic and Franklin was associated with several other women during the marriage, one who was even with him at the time of his death.

Mrs. Roosevelt traveled extensively throughout her twelve years in the White House. She held hundreds of press conferences and often used her public image to advance the rights of women and workers and to promote child welfare and Civil Rights. She became a delegate to the United Nations and helped to write the Universal Declaration of Human Rights. She continued this tradition with a daily syndicated column until her death in 1962.

Even though FDR considered not even running for political office because of his paralysis, Eleanor Roosevelt was optimistic that he could win. She said, *"A stumbling block to the pessimist is a stepping-stone to the optimist."* Optimism and pessimism are both mindsets, but they are opposites. Optimists see the positive side of things. They expect things to turn out well. A pessimistic outlook, on the other hand, exaggerates the negative aspects of a situation so they overshadow anything positive.

You've probably met people who find faults in everything. They are pessimists; they are more likely to expect things to turn out poorly or to focus on what didn't go well. Pessimism influences us to take disappointments and rejections personally and makes it harder to cope when things don't turn out as planned.

As an example: Jane and Karen both try out for cheerleading. Neither makes it. Both feel disappointed, but they handle it in different ways.

Jane is an optimist. She realizes that there was a lot of talent at the tryouts with only a few openings. She worked hard and felt good about her performance. She got some good feedback. Knowing that she has excellent coordination, she decides instead to take baton lessons and to try out next year for majorette. She makes the squad.

Karen tends to be more pessimistic. She thinks that she was the worst one at tryouts and that the cheerleading coach didn't like her. Unlike

Jane, she takes the setback personally and blames everyone, including herself. It even makes her doubt her athletic abilities altogether. She gives up and never tries out again.

The good news is, if you tend to be more pessimistic, you're not destined to always think that way. We can all become more optimistic by adjusting the way we see things. Here are some things to consider: Notice good things that happen. Train your mind to believe in yourself and your ability to do well. As long as you put your absolute best foot forward (you tried your hardest), don't blame yourself if something goes wrong. When something good happens, give yourself credit—you work hard, you deserve it. And most importantly, remind yourself that setbacks are temporary.

Become aware of optimistic or pessimistic comments from other people. When you hear someone being pessimistic, think of how they could change their frame of reference—how could they change what they are thinking and saying into something more positive.

Optimism is a thinking style that can be learned. It may take some time, so practice it every chance you get. Remember, it's all in how you view each and every situation. So, how do you want to spend your life—looking for the positives or the negatives?

Oh, and one other quote by Eleanor Roosevelt: "You wouldn't worry so much about what others think of you if you realized how seldom they do." Think about that! Teenagers sometimes think that all eyes are on them, that their peers notice their every move. That is simply not true. As long as you are doing your best and having positive thoughts, don't worry about what your classmates are thinking.

"A stumbling block to the pessimist is a stepping-stone to the optimist."

CHAPTER 16

Problem Solving

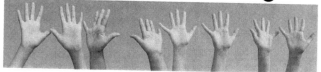

"If I had one hour to save the world, I would spend fifty-five minutes defining the problem and only five minutes finding the solution."

—Albert Einstein

Four-year-old Albert lay sick in bed. He could not even tell his mother what was wrong because he was not yet speaking. Feeling sorry for the sick boy, his father gave him a magnetic pocket compass as a gift. He played with it for hours noting that the needle behaved in such a determined way that it did not at all fit into the nature of events. That compass made a deep and lasting impression on him and it sparked his interest in science.

Otto Neugebauer, the historian of ancient mathematics, told this story about Einstein: "As he was a late talker, his parents were worried. At last, at the supper table one night, he broke his silence to say, 'The soup is too hot.' Greatly relieved, his parents asked why he had never said a word before. Albert replied, 'Because up to now everything was in order.'"[21]

One of his teachers even described Albert Einstein as being "mentally slow". He spoke slowly because he tried out entire sentences in his head to get them right before he spoke out loud. As a teen, he was expelled from school.

In 1895, at the age of 17, Albert Einstein applied for early admission into the Swiss Federal Polytechnical School. He passed the math and science sections of the entrance exam, but failed the rest (history, languages, geography, etc.)! Einstein had to go to a trade school before he retook the exam and was finally admitted a year later.

Einstein finished his studies and applied for the job as an assistant at the Polytechnic and at various other universities. He was not hired. Over a year later, he finally landed a job at the Swiss Patent Office.

He worked at the Patent Office and also on his doctorial degree. His application for the doctorate was rejected by the University of Bern as his doctorate research paper was not sufficient. He wrote a whole new doctorate research paper, and it was accepted a year later.

Contrary to what is written in many accounts, Einstein did not fail math; in fact, he was a good math student. He was a visual learner and in his mind could see pictures instead of words. He was perhaps, just different.

During teen and young adult years, Einstein tried to picture in his mind what it would be like to ride alongside a light beam. If a person reached the speed of light, wouldn't the light waves seem stationery? But Maxwell's famous equations describing electromagnetic waves

---

21   Kinnes, Tormod. http://oaks.nvg.org/einstein-anecdotes.html

didn't allow that. He knew that math was the language nature uses to describe her wonders, so he could visualize how equations were reflected in realities. So for the next ten years he wrestled with this thought experiment until he came up with his famous Theory of Relativity.[22]

As part of this famous theory, he pictured lightning striking at both ends of a moving train. A person on the embankment might see the strikes as simultaneous; but to someone on the speeding train itself, they would appear to have happened at different moments. Because the train is speeding forward, the light from the strike at the front of the train would reach him a moment before the light from the strike at the back of the train. From that he realized that simultaneous is relative to your state of motion. Time is relative; hence, the name of his theory.

Being unemployed for a while and not being able to get into school gave him time to write. Until age 26, his life had been full of failures. That's when he wrote and published four scientific papers. The Theory of Relativity described above, and three others: that light could be conceived as particles as well as waves, one that proved the existence of atoms and molecules, and another that explained the relationship between energy and mass.

While working on his famous papers, Mileva Mari, who had been the only woman in his physics class at college, helped with the proofreading. They got married but eventually their relationship disintegrated, and Einstein sought a divorce. He offered her a deal: One of those 1905 papers, he presumed, would eventually win the Nobel Prize, and if she gave him a divorce he would give her the prize money. She thought for a week and accepted. Because Einstein's theories were so radical, it took until 1922 before he was awarded the prize and she could collect.

---

22 Isaacson, Walter. "20 Things You Need to Know About Einstein." Time. April 5, 2007. http://content.time.com/time/specials/packages/article/0,28804,1936731_1936743_1936760,00.html

Einstein is quoted as having said that if he had one hour to save the world, he would spend fifty-five minutes defining the problem and only five minutes finding the solution. This quote illustrates an important point. Before jumping right into solving a problem, we should step back and invest time and effort to improve our understanding of it. The most important step in problem solving is clearly defining the problem in the first place. You cannot solve what you do not understand.

One way of doing this is to rephrase the problem. A Toyota executive asked employees to brainstorm ways to increase productivity. He received no response. When he rephrased his request to "Tell me ways to make your jobs easier", he received many and varied suggestions.

Another way is to look at the problem from different perspectives. So, you have a problem with your parents, for example. Try looking at the problem from their point of view. Looking at a problem through a different set of eyes may give you insight.

The first step in problem solving is to identify the problem. The next step is to brainstorm possible solutions to the problem. You can brainstorm within yourself or bounce ideas off of other people. This should involve writing down as many solutions as you can think of. Step three is to evaluate the options, considering the positives and negatives of each. Here are some questions to think about while you are evaluating each possible solution: Is it practical? Is it fair or unfair? Is it in line with the goals? Is it dishonest? Once that is done, cross off the options where the negatives clearly outweigh the positives. Then rate the remaining solutions. The solution you chose should be one you can actually implement and that will solve the problem. It is also important that the solution does not create another problem for someone else. Finally, chose one option and develop a plan to implement it.

Not many people are an Einstein, so the fifty minute defining the problem and the five minute solution concept is probably not right for everyone. Einstein's position was that often it is difficult at first glance to determine the root cause of a problem. Your challenge is to look at a situation from different points of view so that you can truly understand the underlying cause, which may actually be hidden.

Remember that problems are a normal part of life, that we usually feel better when we do something constructive toward resolving our problems rather than just dwelling on them. You can complain, be bitter and sad, or you can do something about it! You can look at a problem in one of two ways: as a challenge that needs to be fixed or as a burden that you are powerless to resolve. Always take the challenge!

*You can see this in two ways, as an old woman
or a young girl. Which do you see?*

CHAPTER 17

Quality

"Quality is much better than quantity. One home run is much better than two doubles."

—Steve Jobs

Do you have an iPhone or an iPod? What about a Mac computer? If so, you can thank Steve Jobs, the founder of Apple Computer. Ever wonder why the company is named Apple, or why the computer is named Macintosh? What about the "i" in iPhone?

In the Steve Jobs biography, Jobs told Walter Isaacson he was "*on one of my fruitarian diets*" and had just come back from an apple farm, and thought the name sounded *"fun, spirited and not intimidating."*[23] The problem was a company already had the name. Apple Records was and still is the Beatles-owned record label.

Between 1978 and 2006, there were several law suits between the two companies. In 2007 Apple Inc. and Apple Corps announced a settlement of their trademark dispute under which Apple Inc. will own all of the trademarks related to "Apple" and will license certain of those trademarks back to Apple Records for their continued use. The settlement ends the ongoing trademark lawsuit between the companies, with each party bearing its own legal costs, and Apple Inc. will continue using its name and logos on iTunes.[24]

That's how the company name of Apple came into being. It was named after the fruit. About the computer name of Mac, or Macintosh, well it's a type of apple!

Apple has been using a lowercase "i" to begin many of its product names ever since Jobs introduced the first iMac computer in 1998. The "i" was used to suggest not only "Internet" but also other i-words that it came to stand for such as individual, instruct, and inform.

Steve Job's mother gave him up for adoption shortly after his birth. His adoptive father, Paul, was a machinist who rebuilt old cars in his spare time. Paul taught his son about electronics and Jobs loved weekend scavenger hunts with him looking for spare parts. His birth mother made certain that the adoptive parents promise to send him to college. They carried out their promise, but Jobs dropped out after one year.

He did, however, continue his education by auditing college courses. Jobs was a non-conformer who did not like the structure of having to

---

23 Kahney, Leander. "Steve Jobs Finally Reveals Where the Name Apple Came From." *Cult of Mac.* October 20, 2011. http://www.cultofmac.com/125063/ steve-jobs-finally-reveals-where-the-name-apple-came-from/

24 https://en.wikipedia.org/wiki/Apple_Corps_v_Apple_Computer; "Apple Inc. and The Beatles' Apple Corps Ltd. Enter into New Agreement" *(Press release).* Apple Inc. *5 February 2007.* Archived *from the original on 7 February 2007.*

attend certain classes at certain times. Instead, he liked to simply walk into a class to see if it interested him.

Auditing is an official way to just sit in on a college class. Now this may have been a matter of necessity for Jobs because he had a pretty low GPA (Grade Point Average). Quitting regular classes and auditing them instead allowed him to take whatever class he wanted because he was no longer working toward a degree. He was there just to learn. He explained, "Much of what I stumbled into by following my curiosity and intention turned out to be priceless later on."[25]

While unofficially attending classes, Jobs struggled to get by. He slept on his friends' dorm room floors, returned Coke bottles for money, and survived off free meals from a local charity.

If you live near a university and are unable to afford tuition, check out the auditing policy as a way of exploring new subjects and improving your skills. There may be ways of sitting in on a college class without paying a dime.

MIT (Massachusetts Institute of Technology) has long focused on producing the brightest technical and mechanical minds in the world. Check out Open Courseware section of the school's website, for it offers some unique online courses you probably won't find elsewhere, such as a Lego robotics course that teaches the principals of mechanical systems and engineering using the popular toy.

Of course, always check with your parents first before you do anything online. If you are interested in a university online course, you must first get permission; some are free and other charge a fee. You, like Jobs, may be a different type of learner.

Apple co-founder Steve Wozniak notes that Steve Jobs never learned how to code. Mark Zuckenberg, creator of Facebook, became successful because he did learn how to code. Writing code, or programming, is

---

25   "How To Ghost College Classes" http://selfmadescholar.com/b/2009/07/06/how-to-ghost-sneak-into-college-classes/

everywhere and in everything around us. All computers, smartphones, tablets, websites, and even televisions run code. It's what makes them work. There is a strong demand for talented programmers right now, so see if it's for you by enrolling in a computer programming course during high school or college.

Steve Jobs was pushed out of his own company in 1985. But it gave him a chance to work on his creativity and to purchase an animation studio, which would later be known as Pixar, which was then sold to Disney. Jobs eventually rejoined Apple as CEO in 1997 and revitalized the then-failing company. His salary—$1.00 per year. Don't worry, he didn't have to go to a soup kitchen any longer because with 5.5 million shares of Apple stock and as a major shareholder of Disney stock (from selling Pixar), he wasn't quite the starving artist he once was.

Now, put yourself in Jobs' shoes for a moment. A power struggle had erupted between Jobs and someone he had recruited and the conflict led to Jobs' removal as head of his own company. Could you imagine what a disappointment that must have been? But instead of dwelling on his misfortune, he purchased an animation studio and poured his efforts into something he probably had neglected and missed while running Apple—his creativity. Thus, he formed the company that would become Pixar. When you think animated movies, you think of Pixar.

Although devastating at the time, he later viewed his dismissal from Apple as a blessing in disguise. The door to Apple closed to Jobs, but instead of dwelling upon the closed door, he viewed it as an opportunity to work on another venture—the door to Pixar opened. Alexander Graham Bell once said, "When one door closes, another opens; but we often look so long and so regretfully upon the closed door that we do not see the one which has opened for us." If you ever lose a job, think of this quote and of Steve Jobs' example to remind yourself that other, probably even better, opportunities await you.

Another lesson here is to not burn bridges but leave doors open. Jobs left the Apple door open, meaning he probably did not leave on bad terms, because he rejoined the company twelve years later, making it profitable once again. He was an amazing visionary.

Steve Jobs is quoted as saying, *"Quality is much better than quantity. One home run is much better than two doubles."* In baseball, one home run means touching four bases. Two doubles also means touching four bases. But in a home run, you score a point—not necessarily so if you simply get to second base two times. A quality homerun is better because it has value. Which would you rather have—a homerun with people cheering you on and scoring a point or two doubles added to your record?

It was more important to Jobs to create the best product than to sell the most. But then again, the best quality will often be the best seller. He set high standards for himself and his companies. Quality is something that is remembered. There is no question that Jobs left his mark on the world.

Jobs so believed in quality that he had an entire team devoted to packaging. He wanted his customers to have an emotional response and achieve excitement simply from opening a box containing an Apple device. Apple has been ranked No. 1 on Fortune's list of America's most admired companies.

Quality is better than quantity means a preference for better things, as opposed to more things. Think of some examples. Would you rather have one or two really good friends who would be at your side in an instant or ten acquaintances that wouldn't even answer the phone if you needed them? Would you rather have five good Internet search results that contain the information you need or sift through five hundred searches revealing little data?

The more you focus of the quality of your work, the more you will improve. When you do the very best job you can, you are acting like a professional, someone that will be valued by the company. Business people know that better quality leads to higher productivity, lower costs, and better customer satisfaction. The firm, then, will stay in business longer and be more profitable.

Do you want to get noticed in the classroom or at work or at home? Then focus on quality in everything you do. There is nothing that will bring the attention of your superiors more than your reputation for producing quality work. Besides how well you work determines the quality and quantity of your rewards. It is rare for a person who produces quality work to ever be out of a job. A person who produces quality work will not have trouble finding another job because he will receive excellent job recommendations. Producing quality work will be vital to your success, your reputation, and your pay check.

The eyes can build someone up or tear someone down! You can have a quantity of acquaintances where you are only a face in the crowd, but a quality friend would be at your side if you needed him!

CHAPTER 18

Responsibility

"You cannot escape the responsibility of tomorrow by evading it today."

—Abraham Lincoln

There is probably not much about Abraham Lincoln, his presidency, and his assassination that you do not know. So we will skip that part, and get to a few unknown facts. Lincoln failed twice to gain a seat in the Senate, was disorganized, and failed at business.

But he was, however, honest and gained the nickname Honest Abe. Lincoln bought a store at the age of twenty three. One night he was counting the money after closing and discovered his cash drawer was over. He realized then he had accidently overcharged a customer a few cents. So, he walked three miles after work to return the money. Would you walk three miles to give someone a few cents? It was the responsible and honorable thing to do, but we too often take the easy road. Over one hundred fifty years later, we are talking about his honorable and responsible action; maybe it is worth the effort after all!

He was so unsuccessful at store clerking that he later ended up owing $1,000 for loans he and his partner took out. Even though it took seventeen years, he paid back every last penny of the loan. He worked as a surveyor, postmaster, and lawyer to pay back his indebtedness.

Organization was *not* his strong suit. A strong suit means "something that a person does well." Lincoln usually wore his famous stovepipe hat; it also served as a desk and filing cabinet! In that stovepipe hat, he put bank papers, mail, and notes that later became famous speeches. When he was a local postmaster, Lincoln tucked letters into his hat and delivered them to people who didn't pick up their mail. As a lawyer, he once had to apologize to a client for not replying to a letter in a timely manner, but he had put it in his old hat, bought a new one, and the letter remained in his old hat!

Honest Abe showed signs of taking responsibility for his actions early on. As a young boy growing up in Indiana, he borrowed a biography of George Washington from his neighbor. After reading a portion of the book, he left it overnight on a windowsill with the window open. A rain storm ruined the book. Young Abraham immediately went to his neighbor to acknowledge what had happened and agreed to work off this debt by pulling fodder for two days. OK, so what is fodder? It is basically corn stalks that were feed for cattle.

Think of a time in your life when you were faced with a dilemma such as this. Perhaps you borrowed something and then lost it. What did you do? Did you immediately go to the owner and fess up? Do you make responsible decisions or irresponsible ones? You will be faced with such predicaments and difficult situations your entire life. Always do the honorable thing, and if you have done something wrong, then make it right.

Responsibility can be defined as the ability to be answerable or accountable for something within one's power, control or management. It involves making good decisions, and is the ability to act without guidance. The best way to move from dependence to independence and to gain more privileges is to prove that you are responsible.

One of Lincoln's many famous quotes was, *"You cannot escape the responsibility of tomorrow by evading it today."* What he is saying is that no amount of procrastination will erase the responsibilities that you have, as a family member, as a student, and as a citizen. In other words, don't shirk your responsibility because if you do, it will still be there tomorrow. Someone once said that it might appear easy to dodge our responsibility, but, we cannot dodge the consequences of dodging our responsibility. In other words, if you are not responsible, then there will be consequences.

You are your own person. You are responsible for yourself and your actions. Do not let peer pressure get to you. If your peers pressure you into doing something that comprises your values, they will no longer respect you. It is your responsibility to just walk away from a situation that could end up with bad results.

Do some soul searching. Do you often feel discouraged? Are you rebellious? If so, you may have lost the courage to face problems head on in a responsible way. You may have actually given up and found that you're taking the easier approach of rebellion and feeling sorry for yourself, than by the positive approach of taking action to improve yourself and to gain respect. You must realize that in order to gain independence and respect, you must first prove that you are a responsible person.

Responsibility, of course, must be gained through effort on your part. You can earn it by treating others the way you would like to be treated. Empathy means putting yourself in other people's shoes, so to speak. You don't like for someone to lash out at you, so refrain from doing the same. Try to keep your temper in check.

Lincoln also said, "Every man's happiness is his own responsibility." Happiness comes from how you view your world and in what you believe. It comes from within yourself and your beliefs and not through your relationships with others.

Lincoln for sure felt a tremendous responsibility to America while he presided over our most trying time in history, the Civil War. The responsibility for the nation as a whole and for all of its citizens weighed heavily on his shoulders. He knew there was no way he could put off or escape his responsibilities. He is remembered for the vital role he served in preserving our union and beginning the process that led to the end of slavery. He was a man who cared very much about doing the right thing. His responsible contributions are the reason he is honored as one of our most important presidents.

You cannot escape the responsibility of tomorrow by evading it today.

CHAPTER 19

Success

"To laugh often and much; to win the respect of intelligent people and the affection of children...to leave the world a better place...to know even one life has breathed easier because you have lived. This is to have succeeded."

—?

This quote says it all! Slowly read each word. What are your immediate thoughts with each phrase? Can you honestly say that you have succeeded? Are you going to be a success story? Well, you are certainly on the path to success. You're reading this book, right!

Laugh often and much. You can find humor in almost any situation—it's all in how you look at it. Does that sound familiar? We've discussed changing from a negative to a positive attitude and changing from pessimism to optimism. Those two changes alone should bring more happiness. If you are feeling sad or defeated, it often helps to change your frame of reference by looking for humor. Laugh at yourself! All of us have features or physical characteristics that are unusual at best; maybe even funny. How much better is it to laugh about your uniqueness and have others laugh with you than to be depressed about them? No one is perfect!

Win respect. Remember that respect is earned, not just given. Begin by respecting yourself. The best way to obtain respect from others is to have personal integrity. This comes from being honest, dependable, and trustworthy. Your word and your promises must mean something!

Of intelligent people. Eddie Haskell, the trouble-making friend on the 1950's television show *Leave it to Beaver*, was sickening polite to adults but when they left the room, he was mean to everyone else. I'm sure you've met people like that. They may be nice to a person's face, but then talk about that person behind their backs. Intelligent people can sense a fake. Intelligent people can tell if you are sincere in your actions. You may say or do something to gain points or recognition, but if it is lacks sincerity, then it is useless.

Affection of children. Children have a natural instinct about whether a person is nice or not. Besides, how you treat children and the elderly says a lot about your character. Small children will look up to you—be a good role model. And older people, they may very well need your help—give it.

To leave the world a better place. That does not mean that you have to cure the common cold. It means that you are productive and caring. Volunteer. Donate. Thank a former teacher for what he or she has taught you. Do chores at home without being asked. Oh, and be nice to your little sister.

To know even one life has breathed easier because you have lived. You influence others; determine what impact you want to have. You can and will make a lasting impression on many people you meet. Be viewed as a positive force and part of the solution, not the problem itself.

Do you know who wrote this poem? It is often attributed to Ralph Waldo Emerson and even Robert Lewis Stevenson. But they are not the original authors. Bessie Anderson Stanley (1879-1952) is the author of the poem Success. Her poem was written in 1904 for a contest held in *Brown Book Magazine* of Boston. Mrs. Stanley submitted the words in the form of an essay in a competition to answer the question "What is success?" in one hundred words or less. Mrs. Stanley won the first prize of $250, which she used to pay off the mortgage on her home.

There are two versions of this poem circulating, each a little different, but probably due to edits over time. They are:

"Success"
Inaccurately attributed to Ralph Waldo Emerson
To laugh often and much;
To win the respect of intelligent people
and the affection of children;
To earn the appreciation of honest critics
and endure the betrayal of false friends;
To appreciate beauty, to find the best in others;
To leave the world a bit better, whether by a healthy child,
a garden patch or a redeemed social condition;
To know even one life has breathed easier because you have lived.
This is to have succeeded.

"What Constitutes Success"
By Bessie Stanley (1905)

He has achieved success who has lived well,
laughed often and loved much;
who has gained the respect of intelligent men
and the love of little children;
who has filled his niche and accomplished his task;
who has left the world better than he found it,
whether by an improved poppy, a perfect poem, or a rescued soul;
who has never lacked appreciation of earth's beauty
or failed to express it;
who has always looked for the best in others
and given them the best he had;
whose life was an inspiration;
whose memory a benediction.[26]

Bessie Stanley's great-granddaughter, Bethanne Larson, said, "From what I've been told about her, it delineates her character perfectly. She lived what she wrote. And in these days, with our obsession for the material going full throttle, it's good to be reminded that true success is not measured in portfolios, stock options, or bank balances."[27]

Bessie Stanley's family is not sure how the poem got attributed to Emerson, but it was further confused by Ann Landers and her sister Abby, who wrote advice columns for newspapers. They misquoted and cited Emerson as the source. One of Stanley's relatives, a federal judge, argued with the Landers sisters for a public correction, which they finally did in the book, *The Ann Landers Encyclopedia*. It prints the real story.

---

26 http://www.goal-setting-help.com/emerson-poem-success.html
27 http://www.robinsweb.com/truth_behind_success.html

Read this poem/essay, whichever version your chose, often and reassess yourself after each reading to determine how successful you are becoming. My guess is that you will be highly successful!

CHAPTER 20

Trustworthiness

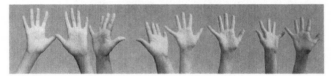

"A promise must never be broken."

—Alexander Hamilton

Alexander Hamilton is one of our founding fathers, but he had a father who could not be found. Hamilton's father left the family with an unemployed mother, who died a couple of years after the abandonment. Hamilton and his older brother were then left with a cousin as guardian, but the cousin soon committed suicide. Eleven-year-old Hamilton and his thirteen-year-old brother were then alone in the world, living on a small island in the Caribbean.

By age thirteen, he started working as a clerk at Beekman and Cruger, a local import-export company that traded with New England in the States. Young Hamilton kept track of cargoes and prices, and often made decisions in the owners' absence. He was such a trusted employee that the owners left young Hamilton completely in charge of the company while they were away at sea for five months. Hamilton promised that he would see after the company and he did not break that promise.

Because he was so trustworthy, his bosses helped pay for his trip to America to attend college, but his work at King's College (present day Columbia University) was cut short because of the Revolutionary War. He served with distinction in the war. Hamilton was such a trusted aid to George Washington that he was appointed as the first Treasury Secretary. He already knew about international commerce and how to handle different forms of currency from his work as a teenager at the trading company.

As Treasury Secretary, he had the insight to create the New York Stock Exchange, where he encouraged investment in U. S. stocks that helped pave the way for the Louisiana Purchase. He worked to restore our national economy that was in ruins after the Revolution. He is only one of two non-presidents to have his face on American currency; the other is Benjamin Franklin. Hamilton's portrait appears on the ten dollar bill.

Hamilton was one of the seven statesmen known as the Founding Fathers of the United States of America. They were George Washington, John Adams, Benjamin Franklin, Alexander Hamilton, John Jay, Thomas Jefferson and James Madison. These men were either the signers of the Declaration of Independence or the framers of the Constitution. Hamilton did not sign the Declaration of Independence; he did, however, have a major role in the framing of the Constitution.

He worked as a prominent lawyer and Army General and also established a daily newspaper, New York Evening Post, the oldest continually-published daily newspaper in the United States.

Hamilton founded the United States Mint, the first national bank and an elaborate system of duties and tariffs. He was also a driving force for manufacturing in America. He had so much influence at the time that when the Thomas Jefferson-Aaron Burr tie for third president went for decision to the House of Representatives, Hamilton used his influence to persuade congressional leaders to select Jefferson.

Aaron Burr would become Jefferson's vice president and then he ran for the governorship of New York in 1804 while still serving as vice president. Believing that Burr was not trustworthy, Hamilton thwarted Burr's political ambitions. Burr resented Hamilton's influence charging that Hamilton's remarks had discredited his honor so Burr challenged Hamilton to a duel, which is an arranged fight between two people. At the time, duels were outlawed in New York, where Hamilton lived, but tolerated in New Jersey. Although Hamilton was reluctant, he accepted. After putting his personal affairs in order, he met Burr at dawn on July 11, 1804, on the New Jersey side of the Hudson River. It is reported that Hamilton shot over Burr's head. Vice President Burr seriously injured Hamilton, who died the next day.

After winning the duel, and losing what little reputation he had left, Burr went out west where he was suspected of forming a western U.S. secession movement. Jefferson charged Burr with planning not only succession, but a unilateral war against Spain with the aim of bringing Spanish Texas under his own leadership. He was tried for treason and acquitted. He never again crossed the Hudson to visit New Jersey where there was a murder warrant for him.[28]

From your study of American history, you may have thought that all of our founding fathers were elitists from wealthy families. Not Hamilton. He basically grew up alone on a small island, but his ticket to

---

28 Schweikart, Larry and Allen, Michael. A Patriot's History of the United States. Penguin Books. New York. 2004.

America and his pass to appear in history books was proving that he was trustworthy as a young teenager.

Hamilton said that a promise must never be broken. One aspect of this is to do things by words and actions that allow others to rely upon you. Trust may take time to develop, but it can be lost in an instance with a broken promise. A promise is a promise and trust is built through experiences and words exchanged with each other. A broken promise then means that the trust the other person had in you has been crushed.

Before promising something, even to yourself, analyze whether you can keep it. Therefore, never make a promise you don't intend to fulfill. The promise may seem small or insignificant to you, but the truth is you are letting someone else down when you break a promise to him, and it may be a big deal to that person. If you fail to live up to your promises, then people will lose trust in you.

Remember that trust is a two-way street. If you want others to trust you, then you must trust them as well. It is also something to be valued because in order to fix broken trust, both sides must want it back and it would have to be earned. Once broken, you can never force a person to trust you again.

When your actions follow your words you are building good character and forming strong bonds with others. When you say something and then don't follow through, friendships will probably be short-lived because others will tire of your deceptions and broken promises. A trustworthy person keeps his word. A trustworthy person does what he says he will do.

CHAPTER 21

Ultimate Ambition

"When I was young, my ambition was to be one of the
people who made a difference in this world. My hope is to
leave the world a little better for having been there."

—Jim Henson

J im Henson's ultimate ambition was not to be a puppeteer.
What he wanted more than anything was to work in television,
preferably as a stage designer or art director. "But when a local
TV show advertised an opening for puppeteers, Henson—who was
still in high school—built two puppets, taught himself how to perform
with them, and got the job. "I never played with puppets or had any
interest in them," Henson said later. "It was just a means to an end." It

was a means that worked—and once he got on TV, he would redefine puppetry for television and films over the next thirty years."[29]

Born in a small Mississippi town, Henson was drawn to the arts at a young age. He was close to his maternal grandmother, a painter, quilter, and seamstress; she encouraged his creative passions and taught him to appreciate the value of visual imagery. When he was in fifth grade, his family moved to a suburb of Washington, D.C.

His family did not get their first television set until 1950, when Jim Henson was about fourteen years old. Until then, he and his family listened to radio shows. "I absolutely loved television...I loved the idea that what you saw was taking place somewhere else at the same time....I immediately wanted to work in television."[30]

Then as a high school student, he got a job on the *Junior Good Morning Show* earning ten dollars a day. The show only lasted a few weeks; and when it ended, he took his puppet show to other stations and earned spots on a few little local shows. The following fall he entered college where he took art classes thinking he might become a commercial artist.

As a freshman at the University of Maryland, he turned professional when a local NBC affiliate hired him to do his own show, a five-minute late-night show called "*Sam and Friends*." His first performing partner would later become his wife. Success on this show led to work in commercials. Then the couple moved to New York City, where his career took off.

In creating his craft, Henson rejected the painted wood appearance of most puppets of the period because they were not sufficiently expressive of emotion. Instead, he made his puppets out of flexible,

29 Jones, Brian Jay; *Jim Henson—The Biography* (http://parade.com/155615/ parade/6-things-you-didnt-know-about-jim-henson-and-his-muppets/

30 "Jim Henson The Early Years" http://www.angelfire.com/me3/muppets/ JimEarlyYears.html

fabric-covered foam rubber, giving them large mouths that allowed emotion to be displayed.

With the premiere in 1969 of *Sesame Street*, the Hensons' puppets reached superstardom. The *Sesame Street* show taught preschoolers about letters, numbers, and social values. Henson and his creative team created Oscar the Grouch, Bert and Ernie, Grover, Cookie Monster, and Big Bird, each with a distinctive personality. It was so popular that it won three Emmys in its first season. Big Bird was even on the cover of Time Magazine.

With *Sesame Street* now in its 46th season, it is the longest running children's television show in American history. Original episodes are still being filmed each and every year. Currently, the cast of Muppets, which has mushroomed over the decades, will be pared down to focus on a core of six: Elmo, Cookie Monster, Abby Cadabby, Grover, Big Bird, and Oscar. The others will still be on the show, but the core cast will be the daily focus.

Sesame Street paved the way for Henson's next television production, *The Muppet Show*, a weekly variety show hosted by Kermit the Frog and guest starring live actors and celebrities. Premiering in 1976, the show was an immediate success. *The Muppet Show* had 235 million viewers in 106 countries. At one time, it was the most popular show in the world. Jim Henson wanted the show to end during the peak of its popularity and creativity—and it did. The final year, 1981, featured the highest Nielsen ratings of its existence.

Miss Piggy, originating in 1974, is much younger than her heartthrob Kermit the Frog. An early version of Kermit appeared in 1955, in the *Sam and Friends* show. It was created from a green ladies' coat that Henson's mother had thrown in the trash can, and two ping-pong balls for eyes. The early Kermit was a sort of lizard-like creature; Kermit's first appearance as a frog was in the television special *Hey Cinderella* in 1969, and he's been a frog ever since.

Then Kermit started appearing in *Sesame Street*, often as a news reporter interviewing nursery rhyme characters. Jim Henson himself was the voice of Kermit the Frog until Henson's sudden death in 1990. Now, let's recap an event in Jim Henson's life that occurred when he was about your age. He was seventeen years old and saw an advertisement for a children's puppet television show. Although he was artistic, he did not know much about puppets, so he went to the library where he checked out a book on how to construct and work puppets. He practiced and practiced, then auditioned, and got the job! The rest of the story—a legend of his own making!

First of all, Henson looked for opportunities by reading the job advertisements, but he knew little about the job that caught his eye. Did that stop him? No, he read about, learned, studied, and practiced puppets for hours each day. Did his effort pay off? Certainly, he would have been a commercial artist had he not worked hard to get the job as a puppeteer when he was a teen.

The pay wasn't great, but at least it was a stepping stone to get into television, which was his ambition. At that time, he did not know that puppets would be part of his eventual success; he just knew that the puppets would be a means to an end. Even as a teenager, Henson knew absolutely what he wanted—a career in television. And he made it work.

In his lifetime, he established the Jim Henson Foundation, which promotes and develops the art of puppetry. To this day, it is still the only grant-making institution with such a mission. In its first year it gave $7,500 to a young puppeteer who would later win a Tony Award for her groundbreaking puppet version of the musical *The Lion King* on Broadway. This was a way for Henson to help other young people interested in puppets to also realize their ultimate ambition.

Simply put, ambition is an earnest desire for some type of achievement, such as power, honor, fame, or wealth, and the willingness to strive for its attainment. The word ultimate means highest, most desirable, or most significant. Once you have your ambition defined, your ultimate ambition is going above and beyond that ambition to a higher plateau.

To use Henson's example, his ambition was to be in television and the ultimate ambition for that would be to receive an Emmy award for excellence in television, which he did receive—nine times (three Primetime Emmys and six Daytime Emmys). He also won three Grammy Awards and was nominated for an Academy Award.

Your ambition might be to play professional golf for example, an ultimate ambition for that would be to win the Masters Golf Tournament. An ambition might be to become a good athletic; an ultimate ambition would be to win the Olympic Gold Medal.

What is your ambition? You must define it now. It can be as broad as "television" or as specific as a "neonatal neurosurgeon". Define it nonetheless. It should come to mind fairly easily as it will be a goal that means something to you. It will be tied to your interests, your talents, and your abilities.

Now, what is your ultimate ambition? That is, to be the best of the best. Don't be afraid to think big. The objective is not to be satisfied with just a job or a career, strive for the top—work toward achieving your ultimate ambition.

Next, think about what obstacles may be in your way. Be realistic but at the same time optimistic that you can overcome these obstacles. This is where you will need help from a trusted adult. Ask for guidance and suggestions.

Jim Henson said, "When I was young, my ambition was to be one of the people who made a difference in this world. My hope is to leave the world a little better for having been there." Making a difference in the world does not mean being satisfied with mediocre or average; it goes much further than that. Through his puppets, Henson has put a smile on many faces. That is to have succeeded!

CHAPTER 22

Vision

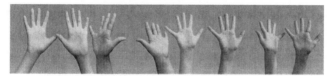

"The only thing worse than being blind is having sight but no vision."

—Helen Keller

I n June of 1880, Helen Keller was born in Tuscumbia, Alabama, a perfectly normal, happy child. But an illness, thought to be Scarlet Fever, at age 19 months left Keller blind and deaf and barely able to communicate. Now think about that, you have to hear to learn how to speak, and you have to see to learn to read and write. So how can a person who cannot see, hear, read, write, or speak learn about the world around her? Keller was extremely intelligent and tried to understand her surroundings through touch, smell and taste. Around the age of six, Keller felt family members' mouths, and began to realize that they communicated by speaking. Being unable to participate, she flew into a rage.

Her parents consulted with Alexander Graham Bell, who worked with the deaf, and he suggested they hire Anne Sullivan, who was partially blind herself, as Helen's teacher. This decision would change her life forever. As a child, Keller was extremely frustrated by her limitations and had frequent temper tantrums.

Sullivan found a way to at last communicate with the child. She finger spelled the names of familiar objects into her student's hand. She also innovated by incorporating Keller's favorite activities and her love of the natural world into the lessons. Keller enjoyed this "finger play," but she didn't fully understand until the famous moment when Sullivan spelled "w-a-t-e-r" while pumping water over her hand.

> "Suddenly I felt misty consciousness as of something forgotten—a thrill of returning thought; and somehow the mystery of language was revealed to me. I knew then that "w-a-t-e-r" meant the wonderful cool something that was flowing over my hand. That living word awakened my soul, gave it light, hope, joy, set it free! ...Everything had a name, and each name gave birth to a new thought. As we returned to the house every object which I touched seemed to quiver with life."[31]

So Keller first understood that everything in our universe has a name, but oh, how she wanted to be able to speak. How would a person with her disabilities learn to talk if there is nothing she could hear? Miss Sarah Fuller, along with Anne Sullivan, taught Helen Keller to speak when she was ten years old. In *The Story of My Life* by Helen Keller

---

31   "Helen Keller Biography and Facts". http://www.perkins.org/about/history/helen-keller

(with her letters from 1887 to 1901), published by Doubleday, Page & Company in 1921, Keller described how she learned to speak:

"Miss Fuller's method was this: she passed my hand lightly over her face, and let me feel the position of her tongue and lips when she made a sound. I was eager to imitate every motion and in an hour had learned six elements of speech: M, P, A, S, T, I. Miss Fuller gave me eleven lessons in all. I shall never forget the surprise and delight I felt when I uttered my first connected sentence, "It is warm." True, they were broken and stammering syllables; but they were human speech. My soul, conscious of new strength, came out of bondage, and was reaching through those broken symbols of speech to all knowledge and all faith."

"No deaf child who has earnestly tried to speak the words which he has never heard--to come out of the prison of silence, where no tone of love, no song of bird, no strain of music ever pierces the stillness--can forget the thrill of surprise, the joy of discovery which came over him when he uttered his first word. Only such a one can appreciate the eagerness with which I talked to my toys, to stones, trees, birds and animals, or the delight I felt when at my call Mildred ran to me or my dogs obeyed my commands. It is an unspeakable boon to me to be able to speak in winged words that need no interpretation. As I talked, happy thoughts fluttered up out of my words that might perhaps have struggled in vain to escape my fingers."

"But it must not be supposed that I could really talk in this short time. I had learned only the elements of speech. Miss Fuller and Miss Sullivan could understand me, but most people would not have understood one word in a hundred. Nor is it true that, after I had learned these elements, I did the rest of the work myself. But for Miss Sullivan's genius, untiring perseverance and devotion, I could not have progressed as far as I have toward natural speech. In the first place, I labored night and day before I could be understood even by my most intimate friends; in the second place, I needed Miss Sullivan's assistance constantly in my efforts to articulate each sound clearly and to combine all sounds in a thousand ways. Even now she calls my attention every day to mispronounced words."[32]

With Sullivan repeating the lectures into her hand, Keller studied at schools for the deaf in Boston and New York City and graduated cum laude (with outstanding honor) from Radcliffe College in 1904 being the first deaf-blind person to graduate from college. Keller then made many appearances on the lecture circuit, and even made a movie in Hollywood in 1918, *Deliverance*, to dramatize the plight of the blind. After that, she and Sullivan appeared on the vaudeville stage.

Vaudeville was a type of live entertainment popular in the early 20th century featuring a mix of specialty acts. In her act, Keller demonstrated how she could "hear" a human voice: She placed her hand on Sullivan's face, the first finger resting on the mouth, the second finger beside the bridge of the nose, and the thumb resting on the throat. Keller could then feel the vibrations created by the voice and understand Sullivan's words. The vaudeville act was short lived because Sullivan's sight and overall health became too poor for her to continue.

Besides, Keller had bigger plans. Now under the care of Sullivan's secretary, Keller became a spokesperson for the American Foundation for the Blind and was already a founding member of the American Civil Liberties Union. She then began traveling the world to advocate for people who faced discrimination. During World War II, she visited

---

32   Keller, Helen. *The Story of My Life*. Pages 53-54. Doubleday, Page & Company, 1921. From one of Helen Keller's own letters written between 1887 to 1901)

disabled veterans to demonstrate, through her mere presence, that they could still accomplish great things.

Louis Braille devised a code based on a series of raised dots. Then three other individuals devised their own system that would allow blind people to read by touch. As a young girl, Helen Keller was distraught and confused by the fact that she had to learn four different embossed codes to have access to printed material. She, therefore, advocated for the adoption of the Braille method, which was finally adopted in the United States and Great Britain as the uniform method in 1929—a century after Louis Braille presented his code.

In all, Keller traveled to thirty-nine countries and met with every president from Grover Cleveland in 1888 to Lyndon Johnson, who awarded her the Presidential Medal of Freedom in 1964. She died quietly in her sleep in 1968 at the age of 88.

In the quote, "*The only thing worse than being blind is having sight but no vision*," Keller refers to vision as insight not visual sight. You see, once she learned to spell words with her fingers, she had the insight or mental vision that she could then learn to talk and accomplish great things. And she did.

For years now, people have been asking you what you want to be when you grow up. It might seem like a trivial question, but you really do need to think about it now. To become whatever it is you want to be when you grow up may require steps while in high school or as a young adult.

So, close your eyes and in your mind, picture or visualize what you would like for your life to be like in say twenty years. What is it you are doing as a career? After you've envisioned your future, share it with someone, your parents, grandparents or school counselor. They will have suggestions on how you can get there from here.

Begin now with the end in mind. In other words, begin each day, task, or project with a clear mental picture of your desired direction and destination. If you can see the end result in your mind, then you can make it happen. That is what it means to have vision!

If you follow golf, you've probably seen Jason Day, 2015 PGA Champion, closing his eyes during his pre-shot routine. What he is doing is visualizing hitting the perfect shot. It's like seeing video of it before it happens.

Not only does he visualize individual golf shots, but he also visualizes the future attainment of his goals. As a 14-year-old, Jason Day wrote his goals down on a sheet of paper and read them aloud before he went to bed each and every night. These lofty goals included winning major championships (ambition) and becoming Golf's World No. 1 (ultimate ambition). Most of those who listened to the young Day thought he was kidding himself.[33] He proved them wrong; Jason Day is currently in the bid for the World No. 1 in golf.

Your ability to look into the future and paint an image of what you want your life to be like will have a profound impact on your future success. Try to visualize a successful result for your efforts for it will be your driving force. If you can see it, then you can be it!

Always remember that success does not happen by chance—you will make it happen.

---

33 MacKenzie, David. "The Mental Game Techniques That Helped Jason Day Win The PGA Championship." *Golf State of Mind*. August 18, 2015. http://golfstateofmind.com/the-mental-game-techniques-that-won-jason-day-the-pga-championship/

CHAPTER 23

Working Together

"Talent wins games, but teamwork and intelligence win championships."

—Michael Jordan

Michael Jordan's father taught him to work hard and not to be tempted by street life. His mother taught him to sew, clean, and do laundry. He was often discouraged as an athlete because he did not feel he could compete with his older brother Larry. He also was not very tall; no member of the Jordan family was above six feet in height.

Baseball was the sport he initially took to and played pitcher and outfield. As a tenth grader, he tried out for football and played quarterback. After school, Jordan would play one-on-one pickup with Larry, who beat him at every game. In his mind, Michael Jordan felt he had no chance to play basketball, but he loved the game.

Although his later basketball career was more than impressive, Michael Jordan failed to make his high school basketball team as a sophomore! Not letting that discourage him, Jordan continued to practice and he did make the team the next year. It also helped that he grew from 5'10" to 6'3" between his sophomore and junior year. After high school he accepted a basketball scholarship to the University of North Carolina. He left the university after three years to go to the NBA draft, but he did return two years later to complete his degree. That same year he won the gold medal in the 1984 Summer Olympics.

When Jordan was drafted by the Chicago Bulls, they were a losing team, drawing only around six thousand fans to home games. Jordan and his team quickly turned that around. In his first season he was named to the All-Star team and was later honored as the league's Rookie of the Year.

He also played on the original Dream Team, the U.S. basketball team that won the gold medal at the 1992 Olympics in Barcelona. The team dominated the Olympic competition, beating its eight opponents by an average of 44 points. What was important was that the Dream Team, the first U.S. Olympic team to include NBA stars, gave fans a glimpse of basketball at its finest, and an entire world responded.

In 1993, the Bulls met the Phoenix Suns for the NBA championship. When it was over, Jordan was again MVP, and Chicago had won a third straight title. That summer, Jordan's father, James, was murdered by two men during a robbery attempt. Jordan was grief stricken and it led him to announce his retirement from professional basketball that October. In just nine seasons he had become the Bulls' all-time leading scorer. He played in 1,072 NBA games, scored 32,292 points, and had 5,633 assists and 6,672 rebounds.

In 1994–95, Jordan played for the Birmingham Barons, a minor league baseball team in the Chicago White Sox system. Although the seventeen-month experiment showed that he was not a major league baseball player, the experience and time away from basketball provided a much-needed rest and opportunity to regain his love of basketball.

In March of 1995, Jordan left the White Sox spring training camp and announced he is rejoining the Chicago Bulls, wearing a different number because his previous number, 23, had already been retired.

In 1999, ESPN named him Athlete of the 20th Century, a close second to Babe Ruth. Then Jordan became part owner of the Washington Wizards, which he later sold so that he could make a comeback playing basketball for the Wizards. He played for three years. At the beginning of the 2001-2002 basketball season, he donated his entire $1 million salary to help the victims of the September 11 attack. Jordan played his last game on April 16, 2003 against the Philadelphia 76ers. The Wizards lost 107-87 and Jordan only scored fifteen points.

Michael Jordan was quoted as saying, "To learn to succeed, you must first learn to fail." He must have learned that from his failure to make the basketball team the first year he tried. Failure at times is a part of life and a part of business. As long as we've given it our best shot, we can still hold our heads high even though we might not have a trophy to display.

"To me, Michael Jordan's career, especially during the Chicago Bulls years, is a shining example of how the best teams operate," said Dr. Bruce Piasecki, author of the book *Doing More with Teams: The New Way to Winning*. He went on to describe how Jordan's team members" worked together in a way that allowed for everyone to learn together where they fit while working for the common good."[34]

34 Piasecki, Bruce. "The Power of Michael Jordan." *Cascade Business News*. February 21, 2013. http://cascadebusnews.com/news-pages/e-headlines/3425-the-power-of-michael-jordan-context-five-lessons-on-teamwork-the-business-world-can-learn-from-his-airness

Teamwork is the art of joining others in pursuit of a common goal. But it's not just joining. We don't join a team; we become a team! Becoming a team requires sacrifice. About the connection between sacrifice and teamwork, here's what Michael Jordan had to say:

> "There are plenty of teams in every sport that have great players and never win titles. Most of the time, those players aren't willing to sacrifice for the greater good of the team. The funny thing is, in the end, their unwillingness to sacrifice only makes individual goals more difficult to achieve. One thing I believe to the fullest is that if you think and achieve as a team, the individual accolades will take care of themselves. Talent wins games, but teamwork and intelligence win championships."[35]

Teams must have a specific goal, and all members must be directing their efforts toward that goal. At the same time, team members need to know what is expected of them both individually and collectively. Someone to lead the effort is also essential; it should be apparent from this leader's actions that they are working for the good of the team. A coach will often let a player know when he does not do his job well because it is affecting the entire team's performance.

In the game of football, consider the receiver. His job is to catch the ball and run with it, hopefully for a touchdown. A receiver may reach the end zone every time he gets the ball—he's good at his individual job. But what about the times that player is not the one to get the football? This receiver also needs to be good at blocking other players from tackling his teammates when they have the ball. By not doing so, he's letting his teammates down. Blocking is also crucial for his team's success. Be good at your job, but also help your teammates be good at their jobs.

35　Henry, Mike. "Sacrifice and Teamwork" http://leadchangegroup.com/sacrifice-and-teamwork/

At the end of each year, football fans anxiously await a presentation that celebrates the best college football player in the land. It is named after John Heisman, a coach who originated the center snap and the "hike" count signals of the quarterback in starting play. Heisman coached college football from 1892 to 1927, compiling a career record of 186–70–18. He was also a Shakespearean-trained actor!

Auburn University in Alabama remains the only school where John Heisman coached football to have a player win the Heisman Trophy. Not once, but three times—Pat Sullivan in 1971, Bo Jackson in 1985, and Cameron Newton in 2010. This ranks Auburn among the top ten schools that produce the most Heisman winners in America. Of all of the colleges, Ohio State, University of Southern California, and University of Notre Dame have the most Heisman trophy winners. The University of Alabama has produced two Heisman trophy winners.

John Heisman believed in teamwork. When he retired from college coaching, he took a position with the Downtown Athletic Club in New York, where he started a touchdown club. The club came up with the idea of an annual award recognizing the best college football player of the season. They wanted to give a trophy and name it for Heisman. He forcefully declined and objected because he did not like the idea of an award singling out one player in a team sport. It was only after his death that they changed the name to the Heisman Award.

A high school football team made it to the final rounds of State playoffs; they were winning during an absolute downpour. The band director had the band members head to the bus to wait out the rain. When the band left the field, the football team started losing the game. Finally giving in to the band members' pleas that their football team needed them, the director let them again play their instruments in the rain. They started playing the moment they walked off the bus, and wouldn't you know it, when the team heard them, the game turned around again and they won! Get involved. No matter the part, your participation is important.

A team can achieve what individual members alone cannot, and all members can reap the benefits of success. Just as it is important in sports, teamwork is also a necessary part of home, school, and work.

You don't have to play sports to be part of a team. At home, working together reminds us that each member of the family has value and that the family unit requires cooperation from each member to function. Each one has a role to play and a job to do. If you fail to complete your chore, then you're letting the team down and setting the household up for dysfunction.

With school projects, working together as a team helps you get the job done with less effort than one alone can accomplish. Each team member will bring certain strengths and skills to the team. The team will be more successful if strengths of each team member are utilized.

At work, team members are often called coworkers; but they are still team members. Every member of an organization or a company will work together for the common good of all. Begin by knowing yourself and your work style. Considering your strengths and weaknesses, where do you fit into the team?

"Talent wins games, but teamwork and intelligence win championships."

CHAPTER 24

Excuses

"It is better to offer no excuse than a bad one."
—George Washington

Although he never received more than an elementary school education, a young George Washington was gifted at mathematics. He became a surveyor at the young age of sixteen and traveled deep into the American wilderness for weeks at a time surveying the land.

It was his military leadership during the American Revolution that insured his election as the first President of the United States. Keenly aware that his conduct as President would set precedents for the future of the office, he was careful to do a good job.

Known as the "Father of our Nation," Washington almost single-handedly created a new government by shaping its departments and political practices. Although he badly wanted to retire after the first term, Washington was unanimously supported by the Electoral College for a second term in 1792.

I'm sure there are things about being the first president of the United States that would make a person grit their teeth and want to pull their hair out. But contrary to popular belief, George Washington never wore a wig even though wigs were

National Parks Service Historical Handbook 1956. George Washington became a surveyor when he was a teenager.

fashionable for men. He kept his own hair, which he wore long and tied back in a ponytail. He did, however, powder his hair, which was the custom of the time. As for his teeth, they were not made of wood. Instead, his first set of dentures was made from cow's teeth. Later, he had a second pair made of hippopotamus ivory. By the time he was president of the United States, Washington only had one original tooth left, and it was used to hold his dentures in place.

Washington refused payment for the eight years as Commander in Chief, asking only to be reimbursed for his expenses, which were never fully reimbursed. He had no salary, but Congress allotted an annual budget of $25,000 for the Executive Branch, from which all salaries of staff and Cabinet members, as well as expenses, would be paid. Most every year, George Washington had to spend some of his own money to make up the difference.

Land-rich and cash-poor, Washington had to borrow money to attend his own inauguration in New York City in 1789. He then had to borrow money again when he moved back to Virginia after two terms as president. His public life took a terrible toll on his finances.

We've all heard the story of a young George Washington chopping down the cherry tree, and when asked by his father who did the ghastly deed, he responded with, "I cannot tell a lie, I chopped down the tree." This story was in the first biography about George Washington published shortly after his death.

It is thought that the six-year-old actually just "barked" the tree with his new hatchet and that it may not have died until a few years later. Nevertheless, Washington was a person of integrity and honor and he certainly was honest, so he would have told his father the truth when asked.

A quote attributed to George Washington is *"It is better to offer no excuse than a bad one."* He did not blame anyone else for his actions; he took personal responsibility. And do you know what his father reportedly did when Washington told the truth? He took him into his arms and thanked him for being honest. He did not get into trouble.

Remember that story the next time you are tempted to give an excuse or lie about something just to get out of a mess. More often than not, you'll be caught in the lie. Then you will get into trouble for lying. If you tell the truth to begin with, the authority figure will give you credit for not giving lame excuses and, depending upon the circumstances, may not issue a penalty at all.

You've no doubt heard the expression, *Oh, what a tangled web we weave when at first we start to deceive.* The metaphor of the *tangled web* implies that lies are much like a spider web; once one lie is told, they multiply. A spider web is full of traps for the insects they are made to catch. That is just as we, indeed, become trapped by our own deceit and lies!

Lying, blaming others, and excuse-making go hand in hand. They prevent you from seeing the reality of a situation. They prevent you from learning problem-solving techniques. They prevent you from learning from your mistakes. And most importantly, they prevent you from growing into a productive human being.

Do you know what you are really saying when you give an excuse or blame someone else? You're saying that you're a victim, that you are not in control of your actions, and that you shouldn't be held accountable, that someone else should pay for what you did. Keep in mind that you will make mistakes throughout your life; everyone does. But it won't be the end of the world.

If you do make a mistake, man up, and take responsibility for it. If you start now blaming others for your actions, it will continue throughout your life and you will be stuck in neutral. Make no doubt about it; if you blame others for your own actions, then you will have a tough time in this life! You will never have self-satisfaction, because in blaming others, you are not developing your own potential.

Remember the definition of responsibility? Simply put, responsibility is the process of making choices and then accepting the consequences of those choices. If the consequence is a good one, then you will learn to make a similar choice in the future. If the consequence is a bad one, then you will know better next time. Either way, you will learn and grow from the experience. But you will never have that opportunity if you do the 'excuse use' or play the 'blame game'. So, don't give blame, get better!

Decide now if you're going to be a winner or a loser! Winners admit when they're wrong and make changes, while losers blame others or offer excuses. Don't be an excuse giver; instead, be a responsibility taker. So, the next time you are tempted to tell your teacher that your dog ate your homework, think twice!

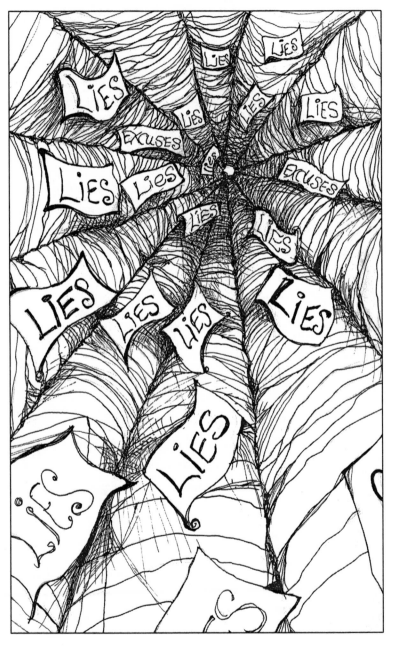

What a tangled web we weave when at first we start to deceive.

CHAPTER 25

Yourself

"Love yourself first and everything else will fall into line."
—Lucille Ball

K nown simply as Lucy to generations of television viewers who delighted in her humor, Lucille Ball was also a serious actress and successful businesswoman. If you ever get the chance to watch a rerun of the "I Love Lucy" show, be sure to do so. It was humor at its best. The show first aired on October 15, 1951 and within six months was number one. It ran for six seasons and won over twenty awards.

From the likes of the show, you would think that Lucy was a fearless and bold natural-born actress. The fact is she was tremendously shy and her participation in theatre and dance school in New York at age fifteen was a complete and utter failure. The school even told her mother she was wasting her money. Lucy withdrew and went back to regular high school.

She returned to New York City a few years later and found some acting parts but nothing materialized, so she took at job at a drug store and did some modeling work until a severe bout with rheumatoid arthritis, swelling of the joints, caused her to return home again. She spent two years in a wheelchair.

She then returned to The Big Apple a few years later and success was a little easier the third time around, but it still took fifteen years to finally achieve stardom. When she volunteered to take a pie in the face during the filming of a 1933 movie, a legendary director is said to have commented, "Get that girl's name. That's the one who will make it."[36]

Now no one is expected to be humiliated with a pie being thrown in her face. The fact that Lucy volunteered for that caused her to receive notice as an actress because she was willing to go above and beyond what was expected of her. That is success in the making! Make a mental note of that—a willingness to go an extra step or doing something that may not be in your job description will be noticed by your superiors.

She married Desi Arnez in 1940, but they were separated for much of the first ten years of their marriage because of Arnez's travels. Determined to work together and to save their marriage, Lucy and Desi, along with some other writers, co-wrote the "I Love Lucy" show and borrowed $5,000 to start Desilu Productions. After the couple divorced in 1960, Lucy bought out Arnez and then later sold the production company for a reported $18 million.

As a young person, Lucy was told by producers that she was too shy to succeed on stage, yet she went on become one of the most famous

36   Encyclopedia of World Biography. http://www.notablebiographies.com/Ba-Be/
     Ball-Lucille.html#ixzz3rJUkaDjW

actresses and comedians of all time. It's quite possible that humor may have been her way of dealing with insecurities or perhaps shyness was just a phase Lucy was going through at the time.

We've all suffered from shyness at one time or another and have gone through awkward stages—the times you thought your nose was too big for your face moments. Others may have teased you or even made fun of you. Although uncomfortable, going through an awkward stage forces you to get to know and appreciate yourself for who you are on the inside.

There will be many phases and stages you will pass by on your journey to adulthood. There will be forks in the road and roadblocks along the way. But each phase you go through will surely end, and you'll reach your destination. Lucy had to try different things before she found her niche.

Think of a butterfly. A butterfly starts as a small egg usually laid on the leaves of plants. When the eggs hatch, they are caterpillars whose sole purpose is to eat and eat so they can grow quickly. They will shed their outgrown skin several times. Caterpillars are short, stubby, ugly, and have no wings at all. But they are undergoing a change called 'metamorphosis' to become the beautiful butterflies that will soon emerge.

The Ugly Duckling is a fairy tale by author Hans Christian Andersen. The story tells of a homely little bird in a barnyard that suffered abuse from the others around him until, much to his delight and to the surprise of others, he matured into a beautiful swan, the most beautiful bird of all.

You, too, will go through a metamorphosis. As Lucille Ball once said, "Love yourself first and everything else falls into line." Focus on being the best you can be and the rest will work itself out naturally. Don't worry if it's not happening right now. Be patient. The butterfly's and swan's transformations did not happen overnight.

Lucy had a bad experience at her first acting school. It's unfortunate that many people retain horrible memories of high school, in large part due to the teasing and bullying they experienced or the gawky phase they were going through. Teenage bullying is a very real problem in schools. And it isn't always physical. There are many different types of bullying, including verbal, emotional, social, and cyber bullying.

Bullying is constant teasing, using demeaning language, or saying belittling things with the intent to hurt someone else, to humiliate her, or make her feel inadequate. It's done with the intention of bringing another person down.

People in popular groups or cliques often bully people they categorize as different by gossiping about them or ridiculing them. Many bullies share some common characteristics—they like to dominate others and are generally focused on themselves. Sometimes, they have no empathy or feelings for others. If you find yourself picking on another student, stop! Never put someone else down to make yourself feel more powerful.

Bullying stops us from being who we want to be, and prevents us from expressing ourselves freely, and might even make us feel unsafe. If you are being bullied, say something! If you are the one bullying others, it's not cool!

How do you prevent being bullied? Always seek friends who are supportive and kind. What do you do if you are being bullied? Tell a trusted adult. Remember, no one has the right to push another person around—period, end of sentence!

People who are confident in themselves are less likely to be bullied because bullies look for insecure individuals to pick on. You find confidence in fully understand yourself—the good, the bad, and the indifferent. Isn't it strange that we spend more time trying to figure out others, and even judging them, than we do in trying to know and understand ourselves?

You can't reach your full potential until you know who you are and where you want to go. Time spent analyzing your inner emotional and mental workings is time well spent. Do that by deciding what motivates you and where your emotions come from, and also deciding what causes you to become upset or angry. These are all products of our mental image of the world formed during critical childhood years.

Understanding yourself will help you see why you are the person you are; it will help you change or control your behavior in a more productive way. That is not to say that you should change yourself, only that you should understand yourself and what makes you tick. And then be happy with what you discover. You are a unique being in this vast universe; therefore, relish your uniqueness. Perhaps Ralph Waldo Emerson said it best when he said, "To be yourself, in a world that is constantly trying to make you something else, is the greatest accomplishment."

You, too, will go through a metamorphosis. We've all had awkward stages.

CHAPTER 26

Zealously, Zoom in to Zillions of Opportunities

Since we are on the Z chapter, can you remember the words to the famous Disney song, *Zip-a-dee-doo-dah*? You know, it's the song that Splash Mountain at Disney World is based on; you can hear the song during the ride. If you've forgotten the words, look them up on *Song of the South* movie website.[37]

And sing that song to yourself the next time you feel down and out. You may be growing up and maturing, but you can still always and forever be a kid at heart! Never let life take the fun away. That is, the fun that comes from simple, childhood pleasures.

You are about to embark on the most difficult task of your life—to break away from your parents and then to grow into a productive, successful adult. In the process of transforming from a teenager into an

---

37 http://www.songofthesouth.net/movie/lyrics/zip-a-dee-doo-dah.html.

adult, you will undergo intense change. Everything about your life is probably changing, and changing fast!

There will be uncertainty and uncharted waters. As you row your boat through the tides of life, keep in mind that all people, not just teenagers, are more open to outside pressures during trying times. Society as a whole is full of influences—good, bad, and indifferent. These persuasions come in the form of music, commercials, Internet, television shows, movies, friends, and coworkers. Never let bad influences rock your boat. For an anchor, you will need the character traits discussed in **What I Need 2 Succeed**. Christopher Columbus said, "You can never cross the ocean until you have the courage to lose sight of the shore." Be courageous as you launch your boat into adulthood!

Let's face it, adolescent years were probably tough. You may have made mistakes, and your parents may have made mistakes. We're only human. What is important is to let those mistakes go. They are in the past. Visualize mistakes as being in the palm of your hand and your breath as the force within yourself that blows them from your hands into the air to disappear. Certainly learn from mistakes, that's essential, but it is useless to dwell on them now. How much better it is to concentrate on being the most successful adult you can be!

It is the hope of all who care about you that you develop the tools necessary not only to survive but to thrive in the world in which we live. You can make things happen in your life. Get busy, do something. Don't let life pass you by!

And if you fail at something, it's not the end of the world. Get up and try again. Learn from a mistake, adjust course, and sail on! Life is designed to be joyful and we are meant to have an abundance of blessings. If you disagree with that statement, then watch the sun rise early one morning or listen to the laughter of a child.

You've read about influential people in each of these chapters. In either a large or small way, each one has touched our lives. We can learn from their struggles—in fact, the way in which they overcame their problems is what led to their success. Perhaps by seeing how they coped, you too can prepare for the unknown.

There are other individuals in the history of America who worked hard and also achieved great things that deserve honorable mention. Among them are Andrew Carnegie, J. P. Morgan, John D. Rockefeller, and Cornelius Vanderbilt. They were all self-made men who became some of the wealthiest Americans of the 19th Century. Through hard work they built their own businesses and their own empires. They worked in the steel industry, banking, started an oil company and built railroads. For the most part, they had modest upbringings.

Although their work experiences and their contributions to society are varied, they had one thing in common. And that was a burning desire to be successful. They had vision, they could see how things in our everyday life were about to change. And they were ready for the change.

Carnegie worked on railroads and foresaw the need for iron bridges to replace wooden ones and formed a company to make them. Carnegie once said, "Think of yourself as on the threshold of unparalleled success. A whole, clear, glorious life lies before you. Achieve! Achieve!"

John D. Rockefeller entered the oil refinery business to convert crude oil to kerosene used for lamps. He started Standard Oil Company and found uses for the many by-products as a result of the refinery process. Rockefeller said, "Don't be afraid to give up the good to go for the great."

Vanderbilt knew about transportation because by ship he peddled the fruits and vegetables his dad grew on their farm. He saw how people desired to get to California in a hurry to participate in the Gold Rush, so he launched a steamship service that transported prospectors from New York to San Francisco in a much faster route. Then his focus shifted to the railroad. He said, "I have always served the public to the best of my ability."

J. P. Morgan followed his father into the banking business and became one of the most powerful bankers of his era. He financed railroads and provided funding for major corporations. Here are a few of his inspirational quotes. "The first step towards getting somewhere is to decide that you are not going to stay where you are." "When you expect things to happen—strangely enough—they do happen."

As time fades, what we remember about all the famous individuals mentioned in this book is the legacy they leave behind. They wrote quotes that define who they are and what they believe. Perhaps that's why they went on to find fame and fortune—because they indeed understood the purpose for their life's work. It was so stated in their quotes that each have written.

They were teenagers at one time also, and they faced many of the same struggles that you, too, are facing. Granted, you may have added pressures in today's society, but they had even more obstacles to overcome. These famous individuals started out no differently from any of us. They were not or are not necessarily geniuses; instead ordinary people who did extraordinary things.

The common thread that can be observed is their work ethic. They had failures, but it did not stop them from achieving, and at least they were trying. They never gave up, and neither should you. Their secret was not to rest on the failure but to get up and try again! They were independent in thought and action, and you should be as well. They never expected an easy life—it came to them only through hard work, dedication, and a belief that they could achieve.

With all of this in mind, it is now time to zealously, zoom in to zillions of opportunities. In other words, "with eagerness, focus on many chances to succeed." Life is filled with many opportunities that are yours for the taking. An opportunity will often first manifest itself in your mind as a thought, desire, or goal. Then you may actually talk yourself out of it! Pessimism is taking over and fear is getting in the way of your actually achieving what you desire. Recognize those negative thoughts as such, change them into positive ones, and push on.

Zealously zooming into opportunities means not only that you look for them, but also that you are eager and prepared when they manifest themselves. Opportunities will not suddenly knock on your front door; you must search them out.

If you want to know how to succeed, then, in a nutshell, here is a one-paragraph summary of the chapters in this book:

With a positive **attitude**, be **optimistic** and **dedicated** in all your endeavors, whether big or small. Have a **vision** of your **ultimate ambition**. Always be **yourself**, and **believe** that you have the **intuition** to find **success**. It will require **communication skills, problem solving,** and **money management**. Chose your **friends** wisely and always take time for family. **Explore** your career choices but always seek **jobs** that are in line with your **goals**. Take every **opportunity** to practice **leadership** and **responsibility**. Be **trustworthy** is all aspects of everyday life, and **honesty** remains the best policy. Strive to get along with others for every job will require **working together.** Start early in establishing a **network** of people for they will be valuable to you through the years. As long as you always do your best, make no **excuses** for failure, learn from them, and don't repeat the same mistakes. Lead a **quality** life.

It is now up to you! What is your quote about life? What defines you? How do you see yourself? What legacy will you leave? What do you want people to remember about you?

If you can dream it, you can do it!
—Walt Disney

About the Author

Linda Carter, high school business teacher, also worked in law enforcement and as an accountant, but her favorite job remains working with teenagers because she finds them not only challenging but also witty, delightful, and creative!

Most of her adult life has been spent working with young people, from having an instant family of teens when she married, to leading a Girl Scout troop of sixteen ambitious teenage girls to earn the Gold Award, to teaching nearly three thousand students over the course of her teaching career.

From the classroom to online learning, she's been a high school teacher for the past twenty years and has written two courses currently being taught to high school students through ACCESS Virtual Learning in Alabama, the third largest K12 virtual education program in the nation.

Living in Sylacauga, Alabama with her husband Bob, she still teaches online, but her favorite job now is babysitting grandchildren and her favorite pastime is watching them play sports.

Professional organization membership includes the Society of Children's Book Writers and Illustrators.

APPENDIX A

Great One Liners

You've read quotes in this book.

Now here are some questions for you to consider!

- Why are they called buildings when they're already finished? Shouldn't they be called builts?
- Why are they called apartments when they're all stuck together?
- The lights went out, but where to?
- Does the reverse side also have a reverse side?
- Why is a carrot more orange than an orange?
- Why do scientists call it research when looking for something new?
- Why is it when a door is open it's ajar, but when a jar is open, it's not adoor?

- Why is lemon juice mostly artificial ingredients, but dishwashing liquid contains real lemons?
- Why doesn't glue stick to the inside of the bottle?
- How much deeper would the ocean be if sponges didn't grow in it?

APPENDIX B

Riddles

1. Which weighs more, a pound of rocks or a pound of feathers?
2. How can you throw a ball so that it always comes back?
3. A large, brown feathered rooster on a rooftop lays an egg. Will it roll to the right or to the left?
4. What is worse than finding a worm in an apple?
5. What is the difference between a new dime and an old penny?
6. When is a penny more than a dime?
7. A man had 12 sheep. All but 9 died. How many sheep did he have left?
8. If 5 cats catch 5 mice in 5 minutes, how long will it take one cat to catch a mouse?
9. What comes once in a minute, twice in a moment, but never in a thousand years?
10. How many months have 28 days?

11. Beth's mother has three daughters. One is called Lara, the other one is Sara. What is the name of the third daughter?

12. I am an odd number. Take away one letter and I become even. What number am I?

13. Using only addition, how do you add eight 8's and get the number 1000?

14. How do dog catchers get paid?

15. What invention lets you look right through a wall?

16. A bat and a ball cost $1.10. The bat costs one dollar more than the ball. How much does the ball cost?

17. A clerk at a butcher shop stands five feet ten inches tall and wears size 13 sneakers. What does he weigh?

18. How many times can you subtract the number two from the number fifty?

19. I'm where yesterday follows today, and tomorrow's in the middle. What am I?

20. What did the triangle say to the circle?

APPENDIX B

Answers to Riddles

1. They both weigh the same.
2. Straight up; gravity will bring the ball back down.
3. Neither, roosters don't lay eggs.
4. Finding half a worm in an apple.
5. Nine cents.
6. When you weight them.
7. Nine.
8. Five minutes.
9. The letter M.
10. Twelve; all months have 28 days.
11. Beth
12. Seven, take away the 's' and it becomes 'even'.
13. $888 + 88 + 8 + 8 + 8 = 1000$
14. By the pound.

15. A window.
16. The ball costs 5 cents. One dollar more than 5 cents is $1.05. The sum of which is $1.10.
17. Meat
18. Once; after that you'd be subtracting it from 48.
19. A dictionary.
20. You're so pointless.

Picture Credits

All illustrations are original drawings by Tina Cargile, artist, Chelsea, Alabama, with the exception of the following from the Library of Congress and another U.S. Government Agency (these images appear in Chapters 10, 20, and 22):

Chapter 10. Henry Ford and his first car; Library of Congress Book entitled Inventors by Martin W. Sandler. All of the photographs in that book were from the collections of the Library of Congress.

Chapter 20. My Wife and My Mother-in-Law; Library of Congress call number Illus. in AP101.P7 1915 (Case X) [P&P]. LC-DIG-ds-00175. Date Created/Published: November 6, 1915 by W. E. (William Ely) Hill, 1887-1962.

Chapter 22. Ink sketch of young George Washington surveying the area around the Popes Creek plantation, in public domain. National Park Service Historical Handbook Series No. 26, 1956. This image or media file contains material based on a work of a National Park Service employee, created as part of that person's official duties. As a work of the U.S. federal government, such work is in the public domain.

Bibliography

Academy of Achievement. "Willie Mays Biography." *Baseball Hall of Fame*. August 24, 2015. http://www.achievement.org/autodoc/printmember/may0bio-1

Academy of Achievement. "Jonas Salk Interview." Last modified May 16, 1991. Accessed June 3, 2014. http://www.achievement.org/autodoc/page/sal0int-1.

All Things Hamilton. http://allthingshamilton.com/index.php/alexander-hamilton (assessed November 2015)

Amelia Earhart. The Official Website of Amelia Earhart. http://www.ameliaearhart.com/about/bio.html (accessed October 2015)

American History Central. http://www.americanhistorycentral.com/entry.php?rec=456&view=quick-facts

Beals, Gerald. "Thomas Edison." http://www.thomasedison.com/biography.html. (copyright 1998; accessed February 20, 2015).

Bellis, Mary. "The History of the Electric Telegraph." *About.Com*. http://inventors.about.com/od/tstartinventions/a/telegraph.htm (accessed November 2, 2015)

Biography. http://www.biography.com/

Bos, Carole. "Helen Keller Learns to Speak" *AwesomeStories.com*. October 07, 2013. https://www.awesomestories.com/asset/view/Helen-Keller-Learns-to-Speak

Brainyquote. http://www.brainyquote.com/quotes/topics/topic_inspirational.html

Brittanica. http://www.brittanica.com/

Carnegie, Dale. "How to Win Friends and Influence People." Simon & Schuster. 1936.

Closs, Carl. "Washington's World Biography." *Gwashington.Net*. http://www.gwashington.net/GWWashington-biography.html

Encyclopedia. http://www.encyclopedia.com/

Encyclopedia of World Biography. "Lucille Ball." http://www.notablebiographies.com/Ba-Be/Ball-Lucille.html#ixzz3rJUkaDjW

Encyclopedia of World Biography. "Willie Mays." http://www.notablebiographies.com/Ma-Mo/Mays-Willie.html

Envision experience. http://www.envisionexperince.com/ (accessed August 18, 2015).

FDR Library. http://www.fdrlibrary.marist.edu/ (accessed August 20, 2015).

Ford, Henry. "My Life and Work." Kessinger Publishing. 1922.

Goal Setting. http://www.goal-setting-help.com/emerson-poem-success.html (accessed October 2015)

Helen Keller Biography and Facts. http://www.perkins.org/about/history/helen-keller (accessed October 2015)

Henry, Mike. "Sacrifice and Teamwork." *Mastering Leadership*. http://leadchangegroup.com/sacrifice-and-teamwork/ (accessed October 2015)

Heritage.org. http://www.heritage.org/research/lecture/ronald-reagan-and-the-fall-of-communism (accessed August 2015)

Hey Kids, Meet Walt Disney (Biography). http://makingartfun.com/htm/f-maf-art-library/walt-disney-biography.htm (accessed May 20, 2015).

History. http://www.history.com/

History.com. http://www.history.com/topics/model-t

History. http://www.history.com/topics/inventions/telegraph

HistoryNet. "Personality: Henry Ford - January '97 World War II Feature". *History Net Where History Comes Alive World US History Online*. August 19, 1997. http://www.historynet.com/personality-henry-ford-january-97-world-war-ii-feature.htm

Ibuka, Masaru. "Kindergarten is Too Late." New York: Simon and Schuster. 1977

Isaacson, Walter. "20 Things You Need to Know About Einstein". *Time*. April 5, 2007. http://content.time.com/time/specials/packages/article/0,28804,1936731_1936743_1936760,00.html

Isaacson, Walter. "Steve Jobs." New York: Simon & Shuster. 2015

Jim Henson Legacy. http://www.jimhensonlegacy.org/ (accessed August 24, 2015)

Jim Henson The Early Years. http://www.angelfire.com/me3/muppets/JimEarlyYears.html

Jones, Brian Jay. "Jim Henson—The Biography." *Parade.com*. http://parade.com/155615/parade/6-things-you-didnt-know-about-jim-henson-and-his-muppets/

Kahney, Leander. "Steve Jobs Finally Reveals Where the Name Apple Came From." *Cult of Mac*. October 20, 2011. http://www.

cultofmac.com/125063/steve-jobs-finally-reveals-where-the-name-apple-came-from/

Keller, Helen. *The Story of My Life.* Pages 53-54. Doubleday, Page & Company, 1921. From one of Helen Keller's own letters written between 1887 to 1901)

Kinnes, Tormod. http://oaks.nvg.org/einstein-anecdotes.html

Leadership. http://www.leadership.com/; page on George Washington) (accessed August 28, 2015)

MacKenzie, David. "The Mental Game Techniques That Helped Jason Day Win The PGA Championship." *Golf State of Mind.* August 18, 2015. http://golfstateofmind.com/the-mental-game-techniques-that-won-jason-day-the-pga-championship/

Morrell, Margot. *Reagan's Journey; Lessons From a Remarkable Career.* New York: Simon Schuster. May 3, 2011.

Motivating quotes. http://www.motivatingquotes.com/

Motivational inspirational corner. http://www.motivational-inspirational-corner.com/

NASA. http://www.nasa.gov

Nastasi, Alison. "35 Things You Didn't Know About Jim Henson." http://flavorwire.com/393253/35-things-you-didnt-know-about-jim-henson (May 25, 2013).

New York Daily News. "Ford's assembly line turns 100: How it changed society." *New York Daily News.* October 7, 2013. http://www.nydailynews.com/autos/ford-assembly-line-turns-100-changed-society-article-1.1478331

Notable quotes. http://www.notable-quotes.com/

Notablebiographies. http://www.notablebiographies.com/

Notablebiographies. http://www.notablebiographies.com/Jo-Ki/Jordan-Michael.html

Oxford Dictionaries. http://www.oxforddictionaries.com/

Parker-Pope, Tara. "Teenagers, Friends and Bad Decisions" *New York Times Blog*. February 3, 2011. http://well.blogs.nytimes.com/2011/02/03/teenagers-friends-and-bad-decisions/

Penney, J. C. "Fifty Years with the Golden Rule." New York: Harper & Brothers, Publishers. 1950.

Piasecki, Bruce. "The Power of Michael Jordan." *Cascade Business News*. February 21, 2013. http://cascadebusnews.com/news-pages/e-headlines/3425-the-power-of-michael-jordanin-context-five-lessons-on-teamwork-the-business-world-can-learn-from-his-airness

Presidential Timeline. http://www.presidentialtimeline.org/

Resources for History Teachers. http://www.resourcesforhistoryteachers.wikispaces

Schweikart, Larry and Allen, Michael. A Patriot's History of the United States. Penguin Books. New York. 2004.

Self Made Scholar. "How To Ghost College Classes." July 6, 2009. http://selfmadescholar.com/b/2009/07/06/how-to-ghost-sneak-into-college-classes/

Song of the South. http://www.songofthesouth.net/ (updated November 12, 2014)

Song of the South. http://www.songofthesouth.net/movie/lyrics/zip-a-dee-doo-dah.html

Space Telescope. http://www.spacetelescope.org/ (accessed July 28, 2015)

Success. http://www.robinsweb.com/truth_behind_success.html (last updated January 12, 2007)

The Famous People. http://www.thefamouspeople.com/ (accessed August 3, 2015). Profiles include Alexander Hamilton (accessed November 12, 2015)

Walt Disney Quotes. http://www.justdisney.com/walt_disney/quotes/quotes01.html

White, Martha C. "Today's Young Adults Will Never Pay Off Their Credit Card Debts." *TIME Business.* http://business.time.com/2013/01/17/todays-young-adults-will-never-pay-off-their-credit-card-debts/ (accessed November 2, 2015)

CPSIA information can be obtained at www.ICGtesting.com
Printed in the USA
LVOW10*2259050816

499268LV00011B/71/P